TRAMWAY
LONDON

Background to the abandonment of London's trams
1931–1952

Edited by Martin Higginson

Light Rail Transit Association

in association with

**Birkbeck College
University of London
Centre for Extra-Mural Studies**

with assistance from

London Transport Museum

1993

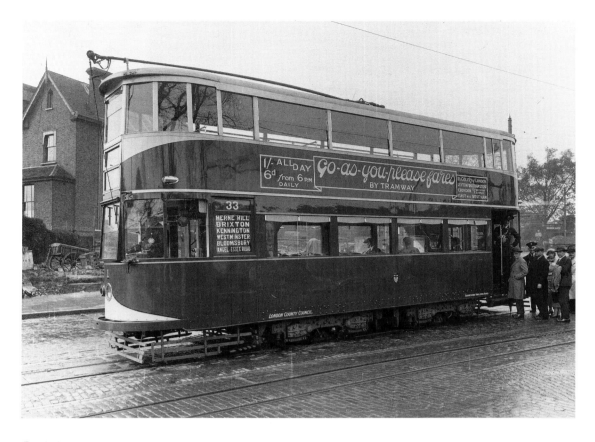

Frontispiece, above

London County Council Tramways experimental car no.1, known as *Bluebird*, and destined to remain a unique vehicle, loads at the Manor House terminus of route 33, before commencing the 68 minute trip which will take it via the Kingsway Subway to West Norwood. Intending passengers pose in the middle of Green Lanes, apparently unconcerned about traffic. No.1's trolley pole lies out of use because here, as on most of LCC's network, power was taken by means of the expensive below-ground conduit system. The date is 27 October 1932.

London Transport Museum 25119

Front Cover

Ex Metropolitan Electric Tramways tramcar 318, seen at North Finchley Tram Station in 1935 as London Transport no. 2255 on route 45 to Cricklewood.

G N Southerden

Back Cover

Pantograph-fitted E/1 car 1172 reverses over a crossover without the need for manual turning of the usual trolley pole, on the overhead-wired Downham-Grove Park section of route 52 (Grove Park-City). Although the electrical pick-up has been modernised, the driving position remains open, unprotected from the elements.

LCC. London Transport Museum 25123

ISBN 0948106 16 6

The Light Rail Transit Association
13A The Precinct, Broxbourne, Herts EN10 7HY.

Birkbeck College, University of London, Centre for Extra-Mural Studies
26 Russell Square, London WC1B 5DQ

Printed in Great Britain by Ian Allan Printing Ltd, Coombelands House, Addlestone, Surrey KT15 1HY

Contents

INTRODUCTION AND ACKNOWLEDGEMENTS

'Tramways, if not an obsolete form of transport, are at all events in a state of obsolescence, and cause much unnecessary congestion and considerable danger to the public. We recommend, therefore, (a) that no additional tramways should be constructed, and (b) that, though no definite time limit can be laid down, they should gradually disappear and give place to other forms of transport.'

Thus concluded the Royal Commission on Transport in its report on *The Co-ordination and Development of Transport* in 1931 (HMSO, 1931). In London, trams finally disappeared twenty-one years later, in 1952; but for the intervention of World War II, closure would almost certainly have taken place several years earlier. This volumes thus commemorates the fortieth anniversary of London's conventional tramways, which ran for the last time through the Kingsway Subway on 5 April and and on the last routes in south London on 5 July, 1952. Your editor can still recall moments of total darkness when the tram's lights flickered off and on as he was taken at the age of five by his father on a` final trip through the Kingsway Subway; and the sight of the tramcar disappearing round the corner after a journey during the system's last weeks.

Thirty-five years later, 1987 saw the opening of the first stage of the Docklands Light Railway and publication of *Light Rail for London?*, the report of the joint London Regional Transport/British Rail Liaison Group on the potential for applying light rail technology in London (BR/LRT, 1987). By the time of the fiftieth anniversary of the closure of London Transport Tramways' even on-street operation may have returned to the metropolis, if Croydon's Tramlink is approved. Why, after being so uncompromisingly dismissed previously, is light rail again receiving serious consideration for public transport in cities?

The current revival of interest in light rail in London and other British cities prompted a re-examination of the case for closing down London's tram system. The question underlying the investigation is 'why, if closure was right then, is re-introduction appropriate now?' This is of course a considerable simplification of the issues, in particular because current proposals are not for a 'like for like' replacement of the former tramway system.

Current construction and planning centres on predominantly reserved track systems, whereas the old London tram network was almost entirely on street; boarding and alighting will be at small stations, rather than traditional 'stops'; and the 1990's light rail vehicle is very different from the former London tramcars. But there are similarities; the old Kingsway subway and the new Docklands Bank extension each serve to improve the integration of transport services; the London County Council (LCC) tramway projections to new housing areas such as Eltham and Grove Park can be compared with the Beckton extension of the Docklands Light Railway.

The four papers in this volume present three present-day views together with a contemporary report on the London County Council tramway system immediately prior to its takeover by the newly formed London Passenger Transport Board in 1933. The three present-day papers were presented at the University of London Seminar *Tramway London* in October 1987.

Oliver Green, then Curator of the London Transport Museum, Covent Garden, London, presents an overview of how London's trams were perceived in the declining years of the system, in a paper written jointly with Dr Martin Higginson of the University of London.

Ian Yearsley, a transport journalist who specialises in urban public transport, investigates the financial background to tram operation in London from the 1920s to closure in 1952.

J H Price, Past President of the Tramway Museum Society examines developments in tramway technology over the same period.

The fourth paper, *London County Council Tramways* dates from 1934 and was probably written by A D Murdoch, the then Manager of the Melbourne and Metropolitan Tramways Board, Melbourne, Australia, following a visit he made to the LCC Tramways in mid-1933, shortly before LCC's trams were absorbed by the newly created London Passenger Transport Board. The paper is thought to be part of a larger document entitled *Tramway and Bus developments in Great Britain*, which was presented to the M&MTB Board in February 1934. The paper, produced for internal circulation and not previously published, was made available by J H Price and is reproduced by permission of Mr K P Shea, Managing Director of Metropolitan Transit Authority, Melbourne, the successor organisation to M&MTB. Mr Shea also kindly investigated the authorship and background of the previously anonymous document. Thanks are due to both Mr Price and Mr Shea.

Acknowledgement is also due to J H Price for supplying many of the illustrations. Many of those credited to the LCC were originally the property of the London County Council Schools Lecture Service, from which they were acquired by Mr Price, who subsequently donated them to the London Transport Museum. Others are from the London Transport Museum's files. Hugh Robertson from the Museum's photographic section was` most helpful in locating suitable photographs and arranging for high quality prints to be made from often unpromisingly poor original material. The remaining illustrations were kindly made available from J H Price's own collection. The figures in Chapter 2 were printed on Harvard Graphics at the Transport Studies Group, University College London, with the cooperation of Roger Mackett and Nick Tyler.

To Mr Price a debt of gratitude is owed for arranging the vital financial backing of the LRTA, which has facilitated publication of this volume.

The assistance of the London Transport Museum, through the good offices of Mark Dennison and Paul Castle, in sponsoring this publication is also gratefully acknowledged.

Last, but not least, my thanks to Josie Charlton and Jan Ford of the Information Bureau at the Centre for Extra-Mural Studies, without whose help with the production and publication this volume would not have been possible.

Martin Higginson
July 1993

1 LONDON'S TRAMWAYS IN THEIR YEARS OF DECLINE

Oliver Green, London Transport Museum
Martin Higginson, University of London

I The Development of London's Tramway Network

London's tramways achieved their maximum scale during the 1920s and early 1930s, when up to 3,000 tramcars carried 1,000 million passengers each year over a network of some 300 route miles. The tram in London was, however, almost entirely a suburban form of transport. Its routes terminated at the edge of the central area at a dozen locations such as Paddington, Victoria, Aldgate and Smithfield. Only the Kingsway subway, which remained in use almost until the end of tram operation in London, linked the northern and southern systems across the centre.

The absence of trams from central London was principally the result of opposition on traffic and environmental grounds in the 1870s. Under the Tramways Act 1870, the consent of the local authority through whose area the line was to be constructed was required; and this was subject to the possibility of veto by a minimum of one-third of frontagers if the proposed tramline passed closer than nine feet six inches from the kerb for a distance for at least thirty feet. Where a proposed tramway passed through the area of more than one local authority, a Ministerial order for its construction could only be made if the local authorities along two-thirds of the proposed route gave their consent.

Opposition to the proposed construction of tramways through the West End of London culminated in 1872 in central London being declared by Parliament 'a zone prohibited to tramcars' (Barker and Robbins, 1963). Subsequent proposals for extending services across central London, such as those by the London County Council in 1901 and by the Royal Commission on London Traffic in 1905 (HMSO, 1905); and the criticism of opponents of central London tramway construction by the Select Committee on Transport (Metropolitan Area) in 1919 (HMSO, 1919), were largely rejected (Barker and Robbins, 1974).

The LCC plans resulted in construction of the Kingsway subway, opened in 1906, but no other developments took place. The Edwardian era proved to be the period in which underground railways usurped the possible role of tramways as the providers of rapid transit links across central London. Although the bypassing of the narrow and congested streets of the West End and City by the new deep level tube railways was in many respects beneficial, the penalty of long access times and an insufficiently fine network of lines and stations continues to be paid.

II The Effects of Changing Policies on London Tramways during the Inter-War Period

Bus competition began to affect tramway revenues before World War I, but the requisitioning of buses during the war, combined with increased economic activity in London, afforded a temporary respite.

In the 1920s, competition from buses emerged again with renewed vigour. Improved vehicle technology and competition between independent operators and the London General Omnibus Company resulted in increased service levels. A succession of political decisions, however, gave the tramways, those of the London County Council (LCC) in particular, a further lease of life.

In 1920, the LCC had applied to parliament for permission to run buses itself, but this was refused. If it had been granted, surely the LCC might have begun replacing trams with buses. The second event was the passage of the London Traffic Act of 1924, which established the principle of limiting the number of buses that were permitted to operate along designated restricted streets. Most tram routes became restricted streets, thus reducing the level of competition for the tramways.

Also under the London Traffic Act, the London and Home Counties Traffic Advisory Committee was set up and in 1927 recommended the co-ordination of public transport in London (but with ownership

Tram Terminus. Stamford Hill.

1. *Edwardian municipal pride. In their first years, London's electric trams were the epitome of modern street transit. LCC 'E' class car no.623, seen at Stamford Hill terminus in 1907, introduces fully-glazed, covered-topped electric transport to a public accustomed to open-topped horse buses and trams. But the same vehicles were still in service in the era of pneumatic-tyred diesel buses and mass private motoring.*
Commercial postcard, G Smith series

2. *The popularity of electric trams led to a requirement for increased capacity, as a result of which LCC embarked on a programme of trailer operation. In this view outside Charlton Works, an 'M' class car contrasts with the primitive prototype trailer no.585, an ex horse car.* LCC. London Transport Museum 25122

remaining with existing proprietors). Perhaps in part because the Committee's report was still under consideration by the government at the time, London was excluded from the grant in 1928 of bus operating powers to the main line railway companies, thus removing a further potential source of competition for the trams.

The proposed co-ordination never took place, however, as a result of the change of government in 1930, at which time the bills promoted by the LCC and London Electric Railway Company had been passed in the House of Commons and were due to go to the Lords. Had the legislation been successful, the LCC would have remained a provider of public transport in London, which might have resulted in the retention and modernisation of its tramways.

The incoming Labour government, however, opposed the plans for co-ordination under existing, mostly private, ownership and preferred unification under public control. This policy resulted, under the guidance of Herbert Morrison as Minister of Transport, in the creation of the London Passenger Transport Board (LPTB) under the London Passenger Transport Act 1933. Responsibility for the operation of trams in London passed from the LCC and other municipalities and the Underground group of companies to LPTB, where they represented a minority of the new organisation's portfolio.

In 1934 trams accounted for 30 per cent of LPTB's passenger journeys, but only 22 per cent of revenue (Munby, 1978). More importantly, the new organisation was dominated by underground rail and bus interests. LPTB was chaired by Lord Ashfield, Chairman of the Underground group of companies, whose London United Tramways had already begun the process of tramway replacement with the conversion of its Kingston area routes to trolleybus operation in 1931 (Barker and Robbins, 1974, p300). The influence of supporters of tramways was thus considerably diminished by the London Passenger Transport Act.

III   The Recommendations of the Royal Commission on Transport, 1931

Also in the late 1920s and early 1930s the Royal Commission on Transport was investigating a number of major issues of transport policy. Its third report, 'The Co-ordination and Development of Transport', published in 1931 (HMSO, 1931), whilst acknowledging 'the great part played by tramways in the past' (para 365) and even some inherent advantages (less noise on well maintained track, absence of fumes, smoothness of acceleration and mechanical reliability: para 366), the Commissioners were generally unfavourably disposed towards trams. Among their conclusions and recommendations were:

> 'We believe [tramways to be superior to any other form of road passenger vehicle] at the present moment in London, Glasgow, Liverpool, Manchester and other large towns where the volume of passenger traffic at certain hours is very great, but we cannot believe that even in these populous centres the present state of things is likely to be permanent... improvement in motor omnibuses in recent years as regards comfort, capacity, design, reliability and economical running has been so remarkable that we feel certain that the time will soon arrive when the motor omnibus, supplemented, perhaps, by new tube railways, etc, will be able to carry the public, even in London and other big cities, as expeditiously and cheaply as the tramcar.' (para 368)

The Commissioners itemised a number of specific disadvantages associated with tramways. These included:

- the location of tramlines in the middle of the carriageway, without the ability for trams to pull in to the kerb for loading and unloading, resulting in both obstruction to other traffic and danger to passengers;

- 'intolerable' congestion when trams and buses operate on the same streets;

- danger to cars and cycles of skidding on tram lines in wet weather (para 369);

- 'the fact that a tramcar cannot be steered involves a greater liability to collisions than is the case with other vehicles, and if it leaves the rails there is an immediate loss of braking power and it is liable to overturn - an accident which may have very serious results to life and limb' (para 370);

- from a financial standpoint, the payment of interest on capital costs which are 'far greater' than those of buses, the 'expensive' cost of track maintenance - including the statutory charge for road maintenance - and the 'very heavy expenditure involved in a complete reconstruction of the track' which has 'caused a certain number of authorities to scrap their tramways' (para 371).

Despite the acknowledged difficulties that would be involved in abolishing tramways and that 'at the present time trams are necessary in certain large towns if the traffic is to be carried with any degree of expedition' (para 373), the Commissioners considered view was that tramways 'if not an obsolete form of transport, are at all events in a state of obsolescence, and cause much unnecessary congestion and considerable danger to the public.' They therefore recommended:

(a)   that no additional tramways should be constructed, and

(b)   that, though no definite time limit can be laid down, they should gradually disappear
        and give place to other forms of transport (para 372).

The members of the Royal Commission did not explore alternative solutions which might have led to a more favourable consideration of tramways. Whilst it might have been acceptable for trams to run down the middle of narrow streets when there was less other traffic, it was not, in their opinion, in 1931. The right of buses and cars to unobstructed passage was not challenged, with trams seen as a cause of congestion, rather than as a means of carrying heavy loads economically of road space in order to avoid it.

It seems not to have been perceived either that cars would themselves become the primary cause of congestion, or that buses, which were at the time getting bigger and more efficient, would not in most circumstances be able to cope with such heavy passenger flows as trams. The freedom of the bus and trolleybus from fixed tracks was accepted uncritically as beneficial to all concerned.

The conclusions of the Royal Commission with regard to trams omit any consideration of opportunities for separating trams from other traffic by means of reserved tracks. Although most London streets, then as now, were too narrow in their existing form to permit the construction of reserved tram tracks, these could have been introduced piecemeal as streets were reconstructed and when new suburbs were developed.

The predictions of the Royal Commission were to some extent self-fulfilling, not least because they echoed popular opinion at the time. So far as London is concerned, the last new section of line opened at Westhorne Avenue, Eltham, in 1932; and the network was gradually closed between 1931 and 1952, being replaced by a mixture of trolleybuses and motor buses (Joyce, 1987).

The Royal Commission's suggestion that trolleybuses would not be a suitable replacement for most of London's tramways, as the latter were electrified on the conduit system, proved incorrect. By 1940, 70 per cent of former tramway route mileage was operated by trolleybuses, including services replacing LCC conduit tramways, and only a small number of services had been replaced by motor buses. When tramway replacement recommenced in 1950 after a ten-year delay caused by World War II, the standard replacement was the diesel bus.

3. *The tramway reservation on Westminster Bridge, with LCC 'D' class tram no.32, at the end of the Edwardian period, circa 1907–1910. The roadside reservation extended along the Embankment, but exclusive right of way for trams was rare in London and tram service reliability suffered as other road traffic increased.*
Commercial postcard, LL series

4. *In a scene little changed in over sixty years – apart from the removal of the tram lines – six trams and four buses cross Westminster Bridge and pass the 'new' County Hall in the late 1920s. The covered topped trams are clearly a preferable all-weather transport mode than the open top buses, but both trams and buses are susceptible to delay from horse-drawn vehicles. The lack of any clear location for southbound traffic may be noticed. The no.53 bus and horse-drawn van in the foreground have taken a kerbside path, whilst the van in the middle distance has chosen a route on the offside of the tram tracks. Such confusion doubtless contributed to the perceived 'problem' of trams at this period, which helped bring about their demise.*
London Transport Museum

IV   A Critical Comment on the Role of the London County Council

Wide central reservations were indeed created when the Becontree housing estate was built, to allow for the introduction of tram services (Jackson, 1973, p291). However, these, along with a number of other proposed suburban extensions (for example Grove Park - Eltham and Hendon - Golders Green, op cit pp248, 72) did not materialise.

Jackson notes that the LCC was not always able to obtain sanction from local authorities through which new tram routes would pass in order to connect new out-county housing estates to the tramway network. For example, the LCC tried without success to persuade Ilford to extend its trams across Becontree to join the Barking council system (Jackson, op cit, pp162, 295).

In one location where a tramway extension was constructed towards the end of the LCC's tram operating regime, the Downham - Grove Park link of 1927 - 1928, the council opted for conventional on-street operation. Jackson (op cit p302) observes: 'Curiously, despite the simultaneous construction of road and tramway on LCC-owned land, no attempt was made to segregate the tracks from motor traffic on a median strip or side reservation as was done in several large provincial housing schemes of the twenties and thirties.'

Despite the LCC's continuing attempts to extend tramway services, its failure to adopt best current practice must have contributed to their popular disregard. A similar criticism may be made of the LCC's lateness in appreciating the need to improve the image of its fleet of tramcars. The modernisation of existing cars did not start until 1926-1927, apparently then only as a result of unfavourable comparisons between their cars and those of Walthamstow Corporation (Barker and Robbins, 1973, p237).

The LCC also lagged behind the tramway companies that were members of the bus and underground combine, London United Tramways (LUT) and Metropolitan Electric Tramways (MET). Following the testing of prototypes built in 1927, 100 advanced tramcars of the 'Feltham' class were constructed in 1931 for LUT and MET. The LCC only produced its own comparable prototype in 1932 and no further examples were built (Pilcher, 1937, p97; Barker and Robbins, op cit, p238).

V   Attitudes Towards Trams in London

The attitude of the Royal Commission on Transport towards trams probably fairly reflected public opinion at the time; rightly or wrongly, that trams were anachronistic, caused congestion and were detrimental to road safety.

The evidence of other commentators corroborates this suggestion. Herbert Morrison, Minister of Transport in the Labour government, 1929 - 1931, wrote in 1933 in an introductory paragraph on the origins of tramways in his book *Socialisation and Transport:* 'It will be interesting to the many motorists who curse tramways to know who started the trouble and when!' (Morrison, 1933). Whilst not necessarily associating himself with the 'cursing' of tramways, the statement is indicative of Morrison's reading of popular opinion on the subject. Addressing the Institute of Transport in 1952, shortly after the closure of London's last tram routes, Charles Klapper referred to the replacement of London's tramways as 'a work which, but for the intervention of war [would have been] completed a decade ago, and a work which, now it is finished, we can only commend' (Journal of the Institute of Transport, 1953). Klapper classified the causes of the downfall of London's trams under three headings, psychological, physical and financial.

The principal psychological cause was considered by Klapper to be the association of trams with 'lower' social classes. Physical causes included the 'lopsided' shape of the network, the handicaps of single track and narrow carriageways in some locations and difficulties in negotiating through running between different undertakings. Financial causes were held to be that 'public works, street widening, public lavatories, and the like were thrust on tramway authorities under the threat of the local veto'; the higher operating costs per vehicle mile of trams compared to buses and trolleybuses; and the convenience of the bus in being able to fan out to serve low density suburbs. The latter was seen as a disadvantage not faced by Continental cities, with their more dense populations and tightly constrained boundaries.

Tellingly, Klapper concluded: 'London is in the British fashion, of course; we now (1952) have only ten tramway systems left in England and Scotland, most of them doomed.'

The local authority veto referred to by Klapper comprised two elements. The first was the power to prevent tramway construction contained in the Tramways Act 1870, discussed at the beginning of this chapter. The second was the power of veto on overhead electric tram wires, granted to local authorities following the assumption by the LCC in 1896 of tramway operating powers and in 1900 of powers to electrify lines it operated (Gibbon and Bell, 1939, p616). It was this power of veto which led to the adoption by the LCC of the expensive conduit system of electrification for tramways in inner London. In 1931 the LCC tramway system comprised 123 track miles electrified on the conduit system and 43 miles with overhead wires (Haward, 1932, p293).

The combined influence of the state of technical knowledge and the exercising of political power may also be seen in the failure of the LCC to obtain the power to run trolleybuses. In 1913 and again in 1922, the LCC attempted to obtain Parliamentary powers to operate trolleybuses, but on each occasion the metropolitan borough councils ensured insertion into the bills of the same powers of veto over the erection of overhead electric wires as they had obtained with respect to tram wires. In the words of Gibbon and Bell: 'This was fatal to the proposal, as there were no means of conveying power to trolley vehicles other than by overhead wires' (op cit, p621).

VI   Conclusions

At the time of the creation of London Transport in 1933, London's tramways were at a turning point. They could have been modernised and retained, by continuing and extending programmes of investment. The replacement of traditional rolling stock by the new 'Feltham' type of tramcar had already begun on the Underground-owned tram networks, LUT and MET. LCC was operating the prototype of what could have become a similar fleet of new-generation tramcars. The 'Feltham' or a development based on the best of the 'Feltham' and 'LCC No 1' might have formed the basis for a British standard tramcar of the 1930s, equivalent to the PCC (President's Conference Car) of North America, some of which are still in service in the 1990s (for example in Toronto).

Modernisation of the system would, however, have required extensive investment in track renewals, including re-alignment, doubling and a rolling programme of conversion to reserved track operation as opportunities arose. The possibility of creating additional links across central London, including further subway construction, to improve penetration of the central area, would also have required re-examination.

Finance might have been forthcoming through the government unemployment-relief programmes, such as those under the Trade Facilities Act 1921 and the New Works Programme of the 1930s, under which loans were guaranteed for a wide range of capital projects during the inter-war period. London public transport investment projects supported included network extensions and new rolling stock for the Underground, the modernisation and electrification of main line suburban railway services (including projects involving the transfer of lines from the main line companies to LPTB) and the replacement of trams by trolleybuses; but no projects on tramways themselves.

Instead of modernisation, LPTB quickly embarked on a programme of phased closure, which occupied the years 1935 - 1940, when trams were mostly replaced by trolleybuses, and 1950 - 1952, with replacement by diesel buses. But for the interruption caused by World War II, closure would presumably have been completed circa 1942, with trolleybuses also replacing most of the tram routes closed in 1950 - 1952.

5. *If the recommendations of the 1905 Royal Commission on London Traffic had been implemented, the Kingsway Subway (seen under construction in 1904) would have become part of a network of north–south and east–west tram tunnels across central London. The large scale of the demolition and construction work results from the co-ordinated construction of Kingsway itself, the cut-and-cover tram subway and pipe conduits on either side of the tramway.* LCC. London Transport Museum 25132

6. *At its southern end of the Kingsway Subway emerged directly on to the Victoria Embankment. Ex LCC E/3 car 1960 on route 31 to Hackney enters the new subway entrance, with the old portal out of use on the left, in November 1937. The rebuilding took place in association with the reconstruction of Waterloo Bridge. The tram tracks on the right continue towards Blackfriars Bridge.* London Transport Museum 25130

13

Environmental considerations were clearly an important factor in the rise and fall of London's tramways, being in part responsible for the shape of the network, the type of electrification system (and therefore for inflated capital and operating costs) and consequently also perhaps for the premature demise of the system compared to those of other major cities. However, the environmental considerations omitted some of those now held to be important.

The 'visual intrusion' of overhead wires and to some extent of the vehicles themselves (perhaps most particularly due to their noise); and the congestion caused by large vehicles requiring to stop at frequent intervals in the middle of the road were the prime concerns in the 1920s and 1930s. Although the 1931 Royal Commission report mentions freedom from 'offensive fumes' this aspect of environmental protection does not appear to have been a major issue sixty years ago.

Above all, however, the ability of trams, especially when operating on reserved tracks, to carry greater loads than buses, appears not to have received serious consideration. It was left to commentators after closure had taken place, such as Jackson (1973), to comment on London's failure to segregate trams from other traffic, even when new construction would appear to have made this possible.

It seems that because larger and technically better buses, including trolleybuses, with the added advantage that they could continue to use tramway electric power installations, were rapidly being introduced, they should properly replace antiquated tramways. Evidence that modern trolleybuses achieved improved revenues (5per ecnt higher than on the trams they replaced: Barker and Robbins, 1974, p302) was cited in favour of completion of the programme of tramway replacement.

The effects of traffic congestion in London on the scale now experienced were, perhaps not surprisingly, not anticipated in the 1930s, nor even after World War II. A mode of transport potentially suited to reserved track operation, and even the small number of existing segregated tram tracks, such as Kingsway/Embankment, Blackfriars and Westminster bridges, Whipps Cross Road, Leytonstone and the western approach to Alexandra Palace, were given up.

The new uses for the different parts of the Kingsway subway (flood control centre, storage depot, road tunnel; see Dunbar, 1974) are well-known. The former tramway reservations on the Embankment and Thames bridges have been assimilated into the carriageways available for general traffic and, incredibly, Embankment now has no bus service except the Monday to Friday rush hour projection of one route. The sleeper track tramway in Alexandra Park was paved over to form a road for the replacement buses. The Whipps Cross Road roadside reservation has never found an alternative use, except in part as a layby and for car parking and still, in 1991, remains largely in existence as a gravelled strip.

The programme of abandonment of London's tramways was probably inevitable when it took place. Whether, with the benefit of hindsight, the decision to replace trams with buses was a good thing is another matter. The problem of traffic congestion was not solved by abolishing trams; it was probably only temporarily alleviated. Buses are made unreliable by the requirement to share roadspace with other vehicles. The creation of reserved lanes except in places where to do so does not delay other traffic is discouraged (Department of Transport, 1988).

If trams had remained, their tracks would by now have been segregated in many places, gradually facilitated as redevelopment programmes and road reconstruction progressed. Whilst London was spared destruction on the scale experienced by, for example German and Dutch cities in World War II, the consequent advantage of post-war reconstruction on more spacious lines would also not have arisen in London. However, if the trams had survived longer, they might by now have been accorded at least the degree of modernisation afforded in France to the Lille Mongy line or the Marseilles tramway, if not the thorough conversion to light railways that has taken place in many German cities. Much of London's former network of tram routes has changed extensively as a result of revised route patterns to reflect changes in demand, or new road construction, especially in the outer areas. In this respect, one of the arguments for tramway abandonment, and often for the subsequent replacement of trolleybuses by diesel buses, has been vindicated, as public transport has been extended to serve new, and often lower density, housing.

In contrast, many former tram routes are still operated by buses substantially in the same form. Generally, these are main trunk radial routes operating at high frequencies, such as Uxbridge - Shepherds Bush (much of which route is along a wide, dual carriageway and is now under consideration to become London's first Green Route, with extensive bus priorities) and Waltham Cross - Smithfield. The orbital Aldgate - Warren Street bus route 253 ran between the same termini as its tram and trolleybus ancestors until it was cut back to Mornington Crescent in 1991.

It may be fanciful to suggest that the clock could be turned back and such services re-converted to tramway operation, but at least the advantages of tramways are now receiving serious attention in their new (for Britain) guise as light rail transit. The most significant development is the re-establishment of the principle of street running, with the opening of the link across the centre of Manchester in the Spring of 1992.

In London, the principle could be established by means of a similar link through a mainly pedestrianised shopping centre, if plans for a Croydon light rail network materialise (London Regional Transport/British Rail, 1987). Just as trams were a victim of fashion in the mid-twentieth century, light rail might in Britain, as in continental Europe, North America and elsewhere be seen as a major contributor to the alleviation of city centre traffic congestion and pollution by the start of the twenty-first century.

References to Chapter 1

Barker, T C and Michael Robbins. *A History of London Transport: Volume I: The Nineteenth Century*, 1963 London: Allen and Unwin

Barker, T C and Michael Robbins. *A History of London Transport: Volume II: The Twentieth Century to 1970* London: Allen and Unwin

Department of Transport Traffic Advisory Unit Leaflet 2/88. *Priority for Buses: With-Flow Bus Lanes: An Introduction*

Dunbar, C S. *London's Tramway Subway* London: Light Railway Transport League, 1974

Gibbon, Sir Gwilym and R W Bell. *London County Council 1889-1939* London: Macmillan, 1939

Haward, Sir Harry. *The London County Council From Within* London: Chapman and Hall, 1932

Jackson, Alan A. *Semi-Detached London* London: Allen and Unwin, 1973

Joyce, J. *Operation Tramaway: The End of London's Trams, 1950 - 1952* London: Ian Allan, 1987

Klapper, C F. 'The Decline and Fall of the London Tramways', in *Journal of the Institute of Transport*, vol 25, no 7, November 1953

London Passenger Transport Act 1933

London Regional Transport/British Rail. *Light Rail for London?* A Report for the BR/LRT Liaison Group, 1986

Morrison, Herbert. *Socialisation and Transport* London: Constable, 1933

Munby, D L. *Inland Transport Statistics Great Britain 1900-1970* Oxford: Clarendon Press, 1978

Oakley, E R and C L Withey. 'Improving London's Trams' (1932-7) in *Modern Tramway,* London: Ian Allan/Light Rail Transit Association 'Part 1: The LCC Prototypes'; vol 51, no 603, March 1988; 'Part 2: Unification'; vol 51, no 606, June 1988

Pilcher, R Stuart. *Road Passenger Transport: Survey and Development* London: Pitman, 1937

Road Traffic Act 1930

Royal Commission on Transport Final Report. *The Co-ordination and Development of Transport* HMSO, cmnd 3751, 1931

Tramways Act 1870

2 PREVIOUSLY UNEXPLORED ASPECTS OF LONDON'S TRAMWAY FINANCES

Ian Yearsley

I have been asked to look at tramway finance in London, with particular reference to the part it played in their decline from the mid 1920s to 1952. I do so as a transport journalist not as an accountant, still less as a municipal accountant. When I started this research, the transport journalist Charles Dunbar warned me 'you are opening Pandora's box'. He was right, but this paper is no more than a brief guide to the contents. I hope it may at least show that there is a case to answer, and encourage further research. There is probably enough unexplored material here for several PhD theses. I propose to base this study almost entirely on the electric tramway era. In no sense do I want to deny the technological and social achievements of the horse trams, but they involved capital on a much smaller scale.

In 1900, London had 1,447 horse trams with 14,501 horses operating 147 miles of route. These declined by 1913 to 56 cars on 6 miles and were eliminated in 1915 (Figure 2.1). Electric trams began with the London United Tramways in 1901 and other operators followed till in 1913 there were 2,842 cars on 342 route miles. World War I arrested growth, but further expansion followed and peaks were reached of 3,005 cars in 1925 and 367 route miles in 1923 (Munby, 1978) (Figure 2.2). New construction continued right up to 1932 ('Kennington', 1977) but the extensions tended to mitigate the effect of curtailments elsewhere rather than add to total mileage.

The core of the whole network was the London County Council Tramways, with a total of 1,700 cars and 158 route miles in 1932. It was flanked on the east by a cluster of municipally owned systems: West Ham, East Ham, Leyton, Walthamstow, Ilford, Barking, and south of the Thames by Erith, Bexley and Dartford. At its southern tip was the Croydon municipal system and the South Metropolitan company. Two larger company-owned systems, the Metropolitan Electric in the north and north-west, and the London United in the west and south-west, completed the picture. Or almost so. For there was a large hole in the centre of the LCC network, formed by Kensington, Chelsea, Westminster and the City of London. These areas resisted all but a few penetrations by tramway, and so became the stronghold of company-operated buses (Bond, 1979). The large scale changeover from horse to mechanical traction came some six years later on buses than trams in London (Munby, 1978) (Figure 2.3) and initially the motor bus network was not much greater than that of horse buses, filling mainly the empty centre on the tramway map.

From 1911 onwards, however, bus business grew, and in 1922 the number of London General Omnibus Co buses alone exceeded the total of tramcars in London (Munby, 1978). Suburban railways, initially hit by electric tramway competition, had begun to respond by electrification, such as the London Brighton and South Coast's South London loop in 1909.

The 1920s saw endless committees sitting to try to work out some sort of agreement or control between competing operators and transport modes in London. It saw legislation such as the London Traffic Act 1924 (Barker & Robbins, 1974), which gave power to a Ministry of Transport licensing authority to designate 'restricted streets', where numbers of buses were limited. In practice this kept buses off tramway routes. The period also saw the first covered top London buses permitted by the Police in service in 1925 (Townsin, 1980) and the increase in speed from 12 mph on solid tyres to 20 mph on pneumatics in 1928, and subsequently to 30 mph in 1931 (Klapper, 1978).

Nevertheless, on 1 July 1933 the newly created London Passenger Transport Board took over a tramway network which was substantially complete. There had been some isolated closures such as Barking's Beckton line in 1929 and Croydon's Addiscombe route in 1927. And in the south-west corner, London United Tramways had converted 17 miles to trolleybuses in 1931 with encouraging financial results. At the same time, there were more than 500 cars built within the last five years on the LCC, London United, Metropolitan and several municipal systems (Figure 2.4). These, however, formed only 19 per cent of the 2,630 cars taken over by the LPTB.

Figure 2.1 Tramcars in London
Numbers Operated, 1900-1952

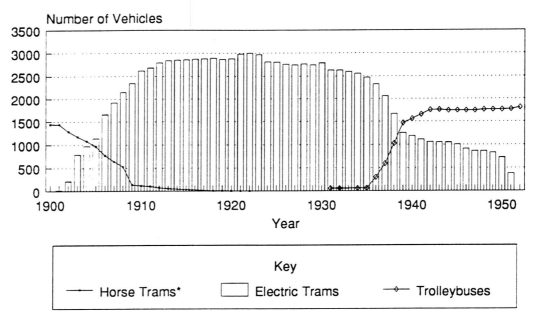

Source: Munby, Table C11.2
Data for 1914-17 and 1940-1 estimated.
*1900-4 includes 10 cable trams.

Figure 2.2   Tramways in London
Route Miles Operated, 1900-1952

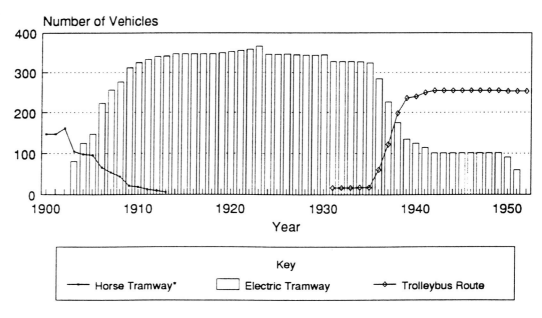

Source: Munby Table C11.2
Data for 1914-17 and 1939-41 estimated.
*1900-4 includes 0.71 mls cable tramway.

Later commentators have said that LPTB started throwing away its valuable tramway assets (Bett & Gillham, 1940). LPTB had indeed compensated other local authorities for their tramway assets, but what was the basis for their valuation? Several of them were given LPTB stock or cash to no more than the value of the outstanding loan debt. Walthamstow, for instance, received £298,460 and East Ham £100,235, in both cases exactly the amount of outstanding debt and no more (Figure 2.5). In effect, the asset was written off. The LCC received £8.5 million against a loan debt of £7.975 million (Dunbar, 1967). In effect, the whole asset of 158 route miles and 1,700 cars was valued at little more than £500,000 (Figure 2.6). Undertakings were taken over on a 'no profit, no loss' basis and accounts were searched scrupulously for tramway funds. Bexley lost a fund based on the Dartford agreement of 1921, because it represented the insurance claim on the depot fire of 1917. A few of the local authorities appealed against the compensation offered, and the arbitration tribunal continued to sit for several years, though mainly preoccupied with the claims of private bus companies.

One of the tramway claims, that of Ilford, gives important clues to the underlying financial problems and I shall return to this. Ilford rejected an offer approximately equal to its £62,901 outstanding debt and in the end LPTB offered £161,550 without going through the arbitration procedure (LPTB, 1933-1935). This represented £99,000 for its current assets. Put another way, Ilford gained £14,000 a mile for its tramways while LCC got £3,164 and Walthamstow got nil.

From 1934 onwards, London Transport followed a policy of replacing trams by trolleybuses. Trams declined from 2,560 cars and 327 route miles in 1934 to 1,059 cars and 102 route miles in 1942, and though there was some post-war reduction in fleet size the network remained at that till the abandonment programme of 1950 - 1952. Trolleybuses meanwhile grew to 1,757 vehicles and 255 route miles in 1942 - and with a few fluctuations remained at about this level till their abandonment in 1959 - 1962 (Munby, 1978) (Figures 2.1, 2.2). All post-World War II replacement of trams was by diesel-engined buses.

The story of tramway decline may thus be looked at in terms of advancing technology of other transport modes: the heavy duty pneumatic tyre which made speed and large capacity possible for buses and trolleybuses alike, and the lightweight diesel engine which made bus operation cheap and reliable. The Feltham tramcars of the London United and Metropolitan systems, with metal construction, front exits and straight stairs, were a great step forward and were part of the bargain enabling the Met to renew its lease with Middlesex County Council in 1930 (Smeeton, 1984, 1986). Faster cars, taking advantage of the higher operating speeds which the Ministry of Transport granted to Undertakings which made an acceptable case for them, offered economies in vehicles required to maintain a given service. But these economies could be achieved by remotoring older cars too.

Upholstered seats were introduced because competing buses offered them, though not till 1926 on the LCC. Financially they were a slight disadvantage, for they reduced the seating capacity of the cars (Pilcher, 1930).

Each step forward in bus design, however, produced clear financial advantages: the drop-frame chassis of the LGOC's NS in 1923 (Townsin, 1980) and the Leyland Titan of 1927 (Jack, 1984) enabled top covers to be fitted easily, adding to earning capacity in wet weather. Pneumatic tyres gave a 66 per cent increase in speed, enabling each vehicle to cover a greater mileage and less vehicles to be needed to maintain a given headway. The diesel engine had a greater first cost than an equivalent petrol engine but much lower running costs: in 1933 the net annual saving was £119 per bus (Barker & Robbins, 1974). Many of the improvements in tramcar design at this time were reactive and cosmetic: they produced no improvements in revenue or savings in costs comparable with those resulting from new bus designs.

There is the question of road congestion and the attitude of the Metropolitan Police. There is the question also of publicity by the bus industry for its products. It is not my brief to explore these questions, but rather to look at tramway finance.

I make no attempt in this paper to discuss fares policies, because these were largely reactive to financial as well as political constraints.

Figure 2.3 Buses Operated in London
Replacement of Horse by Motor Buses

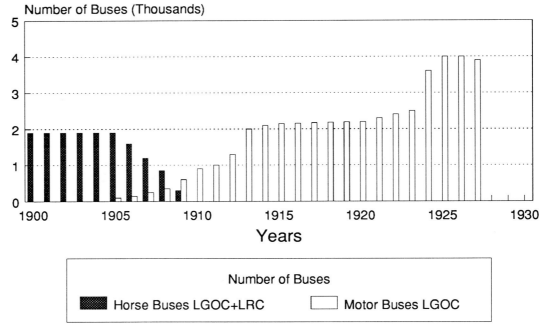

1913-1921 data estimated

My researches to date have led me to the view that a large part, possibly the major part, of the tramways' problems and of the cause of their ultimate decline in London was financial rather than technological or institutional. Competition merely high-lighted a financial defect which was there from the start and would have surfaced sooner or later even if competing modes of transport had not developed.

The keys to this problem are the double accounting system, and the repayment periods of local authority loan debt, encouraged by the division of responsibility between borough treasurers and tramway managers. The double account system was compulsory for railways and tramways governed by the Regulation of Railways Act 1868, but was generally adopted by municipal tramways in Britain. A E Kitchen, accountant of Leicester City Transport, made a plea in 1938 for a change to single accounting, in particular because in the double accounting system assets were shown on the balance sheet at their original cost, regardless of wear and tear (Kitchen, 1938).

The double system kept 'watertight compartments' for capital and revenue items. Many a tramway manager has had to rebuild and repair out of the revenue account to avoid using the capital account which would have necessitated loans being raised. There are many documented cases in this country of cars being designated 'rebuilds' to keep them within the revenue account, even when the new cars used scarcely any significant material from the old cars they in fact replaced. Blackpool's 'standard cars' of the 1920s even had the same Tudor Arch windows as their predecessors to give some credence to the 'rebuild' designation.

The Borough Treasurer (or financial controller in the case of the LCC) was involved because loans could better be raised by the authority against the security of the rates than by the municipal trading department against the much more limited security of its own profits.

Loans under the Tramways Act 1870 had to be sanctioned by the Board of Trade (later the Ministry of Transport). The authority to borrow also included a maximum repayment period. Periods could vary from one undertaking to another, but in 1923 Birmingham Corporation Tramways accountant S N B Marsh (1923) quoted typical periods of 50 years for street widening, 25 for permanent way construction, 20 to 25 for overhead construction, 30 for buildings, 15 for rolling stock and 5 for costs of obtaining an Act of Parliament. He notes that although 25 years was allowed for permanent way, its life was only about 12 years.

The same point was made in 1929 by Owen Silvers, general manager of Wolverhampton Corporation Transport Department, who said that in pre- (1914 - 1918) war times it was usual to allow as long as 40 years for the repayment of loans made for track construction, but the average life of track was about 20 years (Silvers, 1929).

Loans could be repaid on three systems: the equal instalment system, with interest payable on the outstanding balance; the annuity system of equal instalments of principal and interest combined; or the sinking fund system of setting aside a sum each year which, accumulated with compound interest, would repay the loan at the end of the period (Figure 2.7).

Whichever system was used, there could easily be a conflict of interest between the tramway manager, who would want the loan period to be no longer than the life of the asset, and the treasurer, who might want as part of a wider financial strategy to keep annual payments as low as possible, and so would favour the longest permitted repayment period. Given a treasurer who took this view, and the water-tight compartments of the accounting system, a tramways manager would find it difficult to resist the demands of a committee chairman to transfer surplus amounts in the revenue account to relief of rates. Indeed the chairman, the treasurer and the manager could all bask in the immediate glory of saving money for the rate-payers, even though they were storing up trouble for the future.

Some undertakings, such as the LCC, did attempt to provide for the future by creating a renewals or depreciation fund. John Allcock, Cardiff City treasurer, said as early as 1908 that £14,522 ought to be set aside annually in his undertakings (Allcock, 1908), though little more than half this amount was in fact earmarked. So beneath the solid-looking foundations of London's tramways, the 40 year loan

Figure 2.4 London Tram Fleet Replacement
The Trail of Tramcar Capital Debt,
Assuming 15 Year Vehicle Life

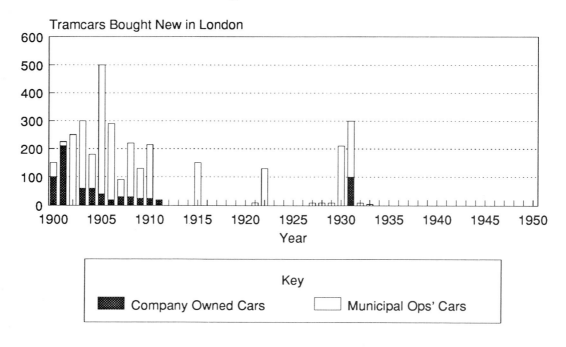

Tramcars Bought New in London

Key
■ Company Owned Cars   □ Municipal Ops' Cars

Trail of Debt on Tramcars
Purchased 1900-1931

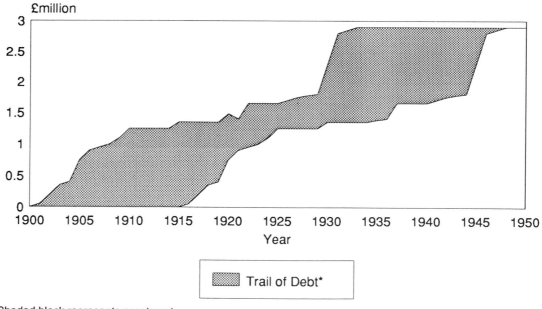

£million

Trail of Debt*

* Shaded block represents assets not
fully written off, assuming 15 year
book life for tramcars purchased.

debts were ticking away, like a timebomb. This bomb was to be given megaton force by the effects of inflation during and after World War I, just at the time when renewals were most needed.

In a paper to the Municipal Transport Association in 1940 R Stuart Pilcher said that wholesale prices in 1921 had risen to three times the 1914 level (Pilcher, 1940). A similar submission was made by the LCC to an inquiry held in 1920 by the Ministry of Transport's Tramway Charges Advisory Committee (Ministry of Transport, 1920). Revenue in 1920 was double that of 1914, but costs were three times as much. Rails had risen from £6 4s 6d a ton to £27; setts from £1 10s to £4 5s 6d; trolleywire from £76 10s to £168 4s 3d (Figure 2.8).

It may be argued that treasurers could not have been expected to consider inflation in the early years of the century. A study of the consumables price index (Harrison, 1987) shows that prices had remained fairly steady since 1886, with a slight dip in 1893. Inflation is easily forgotten in a decade, and in 1901, when London's electric tramway building boom began, it was 15 years into the past. Electric tramways were still a new technology, and little was known about life of assets. Only with use did this become apparent - and in 1913 the upward slope of inflation began.

Charles Dunbar in his paper *Idealism and Competition: the Fares Policy of the London County Council Tramways* (Dunbar, 1967), draws attention to the way in which municipal tramways, unlike the company-owned undertakings, had to redeem their own capital. He says that in the early years 'scraping to meet the debt charges often led to failure to create an adequate renewals fund and, later on, the transfer of profits to "rate relief" had the same effect'. Had the LCC been organised on a company basis, it would have shown a return of about 5 per cent.

The final accounts of LCC Tramways in 1933 state that during its operation, the net contribution from the rates had been £1,294,873 4s 1d. Dunbar argues that this is a misleading statement. I would agree, and my own study of the accounts shows that the amount of £293,592 (LCC, 1928) taken for relief of rates in the earliest years of the undertaking would, if placed in the reserves at 3 per cent interest have been sufficient to have carried it through the whole of the Great War years and to have covered most of the deficit of the crisis year 1920 - 1921 (Figure 2.9). As it was, the reserve fund was exhausted in 1919 - 1920, the renewals fund was raided for £35,115, and the year ended with a deficit of £18,814 to be met out of the rates. In 1920 - 1921, the deficit was even greater, and the LCC Tramways had to apply for a fares increase. Not only that, but it was authorised by the Treasury to change over from the instalment to the annuity system of debt repayment. Charles David Johnson, LCC Comptroller, told the 1920 inquiry (Ministry of Transport, 1920) that this would save £100,000 a year for 12 years to come. He also said that they felt it legitimate to charge half the cost of track renewals to revenue instead of capital account. They had had great difficulty getting Treasury sanction for this, but it had been allowed for 1918 - 1919 and 1919 - 1920. Even with these measures the LCC Tramways were still in difficulties and Treasury approval was given for them to suspend repayment of capital for three years up to 31 March 1927, paying interest only in these years.

In 1920 LCC general manager A L C Fell said that to catch up with wartime arrears, 25 miles of renewals a year would be needed for the next five years instead of the normal 22 miles. LCCT regarded anything over a quarter of a mile as a renewal rather than a repair. One can see the incentive for patching track out of the revenue account! Small wonder that LCC contributed nothing to relief of rates at this time. Instead, it drew £226,210 10s 2d out of the Special County Account to meet its deficit.

Overall, London's local authority tramways contributed nothing in net terms to rates after 1911 apart from some isolated items such as the payments by the LCC in 1922 - 1923, perhaps an attempt to repay some of the 1920 - 1921 amount. West Ham in its final year put £7,210 to relief of rates and carried forward a £11,345 deficit (Garcke, 1934), all of which sounds like a political gesture. The company-owned tramways fared little better. London United had grandiose plans for a network which never materialised, and had a fleet some 30 per cent larger than it needed for all except Summer holiday traffic. It had also spent some £1 million, about 44 per cent of its total capital, on street widening and wayleave payments which gave no direct return on investment. So in 1919 its capital was written down from £2.25 million to £1.6 million. But its shareholders did not do well out of their investment.

Figure 2.5 Municipal Tramways Valuations at Takeover by LPTB

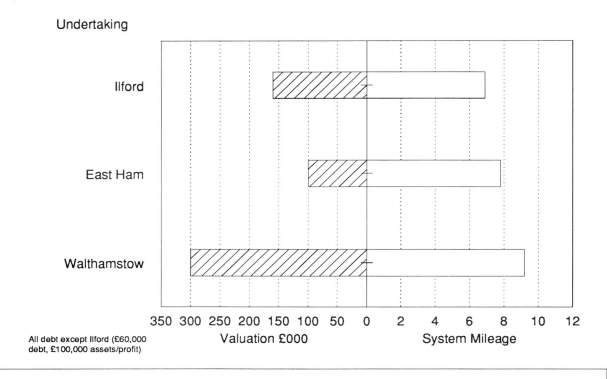

All debt except Ilford (£60,000 debt, £100,000 assets/profit)

Figure 2.6 Valuation of Tramway Assets On Takeover by London Transport

Owning Authority	Valuation £
LCC (LA 5.5%)	8,500,000
Middlesex (LA A)	1,035,000
Metropolitan Electric Tramways (ABC)	927,792
Walthamstow	291,475
Leyton	184,356
Croydon	173,746
Ilford (Originally £69,000)	161,550
East Ham	100,235
Dartford	34,084
Barking	30,100
Bexley	27,500
Hertfordshire	19,000
Erith	4,687
City of London	2,500

Valuations on 'No Profit - No Loss' Basis

Ordinary shareholders last saw a dividend (of 1 per cent) in 1907, and preference shareholders received 0.5 per cent in 1914 and nothing thereafter. As early as 1901 an editorial in *Garcke's Manual of Electrical Undertakings* pointed out that telegraph companies gave a better return on investment than traction. *Tramway and Railway World* of 21 February 1920 referred to the 'double burden' of concurrent debts and cited West Ham at £50,327 and East Ham, at £11,474 as the highest municipal tramway deficits in the country. (West Ham later distinguished itself, in 1925 by incurring working costs which exceeded revenue!)

Tramway and Railway World in 1920 printed extensive editorials on what it called 'The Financial Crisis', and echoes of it continued into the decade. At the centre of the crisis was the cost of track renewals, and it is reasonable to ask what was done to reduce this, both in London and elsewhere. C S Smeeton (1984, 1986) records that the Metropolitan Electric Tramways had constructed tramways at £15,000 per double track mile pre-war but in 1919 the cost was £37,772 by conventional methods. Introducing American mechanised methods brought the cost down to £20,000.

Much of the cost of track construction or reconstruction arose from providing the road surface for other vehicles, which were wearing it out at an increasing rate in the 1920s. On the grounds that it was unfairly being asked to pay the cost of a road for competing buses, Metropolitan Electric Tramways appealed against a rates assessment on tracks and had it reduced by 75 per cent from 1926. In Liverpool the city engineer Brodie had discovered that track costs could be cut and speeds increased by creating unpaved sleeper tracks on reservations (Horne & Maund, 1982). The idea was picked up widely, by Birmingham, Manchester, Leeds, Bradford, Sheffield, Leicester and others. But in London this method was scarcely at all used, though land was set aside on LUT's Uxbridge route.

LCC had a particular problem because the whole of the inner network was, largely for what we would now call 'environmental' reasons, on the underground conduit system. Conduit track construction cost three times that of track for conventional overhead systems, and even though foundations were immensely solid, there was the added cost of tee-rail renewal, about 30 route miles a year being needed (Ministry of Transport, 1920). Track lasted an average of 12 years on the LCC system, reflecting frequent services, large cars, and the use of the magnetic track brake for service stops. This helped LCC and other London Tramways to maintain high average speeds, so that there were cost savings as fewer cars were requested to maintain a given headway.

One system which did not use magnetic brakes was Ilford, an extremely well-managed system though somewhat conservative in car design ('Rodinglea', 1967). Ilford repaid its loan debt faster than other undertakings and felt it was being penalised for its good management by the London Passenger Transport Board stock offer in 1933. It obviously had a good case, for the amount was almost trebled.

The LCC Tramways always had the disadvantage of starting their services from the perimeter of the central business districts of the City and West End. The Kingsway Subway, opened for single deck cars in 1906 - 1908 and deepened to take double decks in 1931, was but part of a larger scheme for subways to penetrate the centre, but a change of political control from Progressives to Moderates in 1907 prevented this going ahead (Jackson, 1965).

In fairness it should be said that the Moderates' concern was about LCC capital spending in general and not just the tramways. In 1889 the LCC inherited £30 million capital debt from its predecessor the Metropolitan Board of Works and by 1907 the LCC's long-term debt was £73 million, of which £19 million were debts due to other bodies. Rigid economies were applied to all departments, not just the tramways, but this was the very time when the motor bus was taking over from the horse, and investment to give a foothold in the central area could have contributed greatly to later revenue. Part of LCC's inheritance from the Metropolitan Board of Works was that it had to apply for powers to borrow money, not just through the Board of Trade or from 1919 The Ministry of Transport, but through submitting an annual Money Bill to Parliament. This could give an opportunity for MPs to give support or protest.

Figure 2.7(a) Tram Track: Capital Cost per Mile of Double Track.

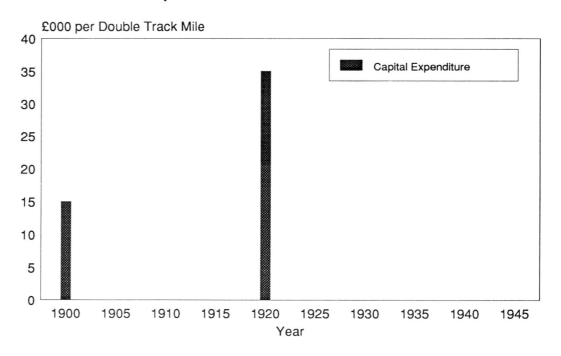

£000 per Double Track Mile

Fig 2.7(b) Tram Track: Annual Costs of Writing off Capital Costs. Effects of Inflation and Length of Write-off Period

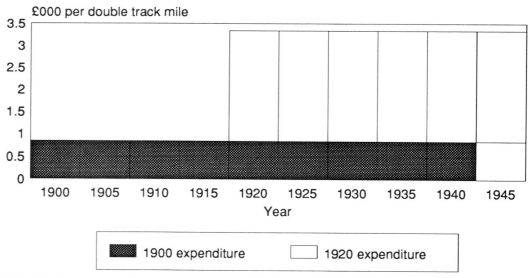

£000 per double track mile

Low first cost: 40 year write-off.
Renewal after 20 years at inflated
cost: written off over 20 years.

Given all these financial problems, and the growth of bus competition, why did the London tramways not seek powers to run buses themselves? In fact many of them did, but were always met by strong opposition from the London General Omnibus Company and other bus interests. The situation was thus quite different from provincial cities where tramways had a monopoly of city centre traffic.

LCC tried to get bus powers for feeder services in 1920, and at various times other undertakings proposed buses or trolleybuses. West Ham tried for two specific bus routes in 1925. East Ham planned to introduce a trolleybus bill to the 1926 Parliamentary session, but dropped it because of local opposition based on fears that workmen's fares would disappear. Local opposition also thwarted Croydon's 1924 trolleybus proposal for its Addiscombe route, which eventually was replaced by LGOC buses in 1927.

It could be argued that the greater part of the £66,000 Croydon spent in 1927 - 1928 in new cars for through running to London represented the £50,000 it would otherwise have spent relaying the track to Addiscombe (Baddeley, 1960).

The local authority-owned tramways had no chance of obtaining bus powers, and the option of selling out to the LGOC was politically unacceptable. So they did their best with the tramways they had. The company-owned tramways, however, demonstrated other options. One of these was the fleet of modern Feltham trams bought by the MET and LUT. More significant in the long run was the LUT's trolleybus conversion in the Twickenham - Kingston area in 1931.

Geoffrey Wilson in his book on London United Tramways (Wilson, 1971) records that Christopher John Spencer, manager of both the MET and the LUT, said that it would have cost £550,000 to renew tramways in the Twickenham - Kingston area and only £230,000 to convert to trolleybuses, including £66,000 paid to local authorities in respect of abandoned tracks. Oliver Green and John Reed, in the *London Transport Golden Jubilee Book* put it succinctly by saying that conversion to trolleybuses was cheaper than either modernising the system or replacing trams with diesel buses, as much of the electrical equipment could be re-used but without the need for new track (Green & Reed, 1983).

Another factor was the wage structure. Tram crews were on a lower pay scale than bus crews, and widespread conversion to buses would have increased the wage bill considerably. In 1933, bus drivers basic pay was £4 6s 6d and bus conductors earned £3 19s 6d. Tram drivers and conductors earned the same, £3 13s (Figure 2.10). Had LPTB converted to buses, it would have added £307,000 a year to its wage bill. Conversion to trolleybuses allowed LPTB to retain the tramway pay scale.

This does not pretend to be an exhaustive survey of London's tramway finance. Many questions need to be resolved: for instance, the precise amounts of compensation given to undertakings differ slightly between sources. But there are major questions which invite research. J Sleeman, in his paper *The Rise and Decline of Municipal Transport*, says that in 1913 the problems of London's tramways were contrasted to a general picture of 'prosperous and expanding municipal tramways, especially in the larger towns' (Sleeman, undated). Yet the 'crisis' editorials in *Tramway and Railway World* (1920) and the representations to Government by the Municipal Tramways Association in 1920, were on a nationwide basis. How different was the London situation from the rest of the country?

Then there is the vexed question of loan repayment, in effect, redemption of capital. National Bus Company reports in the late 1970s and early 1980s (NBC, 1979, 1980) bewail the need to service and redeem the commencing capital debt, and counties regarded this as an unjust element of subsidy charges. Dunbar maintains that the LCC Tramways would have returned 5 per cent if run as a company. Would this have been true of the other municipal tramways in London?

Further research is needed into the subsequent performance of LPTB stocks issued as compensation. These had redemption dates from 1943 to 2023, but most were exchanged for other Government backed stocks in the 1948 Nationalisation which created the London Transport Executive. Frank Pick made a defence of the return on LPTB 'C' stock in 1939 (Pick, 1939) pointing out that loans at 2.25 per cent were available from the London Electric Transport Finance Corporation (LETFC) and this 'bargain' justified the prior charge stocks issued to the Underground group. He was trying to allay suspicions that the tram, trolleybus and bus side of LPTB was cross-subsidising its railways.

Figure 2.8 Costs of Tram Track Capital and Replacement Costs, 1913 to 1937

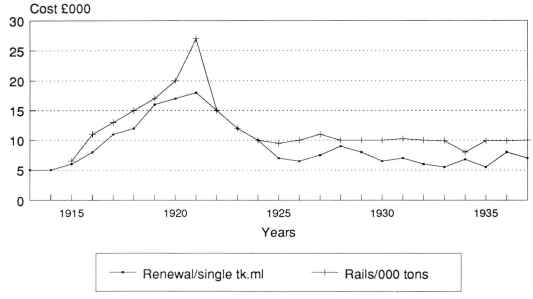

Source: R S Pilcher, 1940

L D Kitchen records the rate of 'C' stock interest from 1934 to 1939 as 3.5, 4, 4, 4.5, 4 and 1.5 per cent (Kitchen, 1939). LETFC is rarely mentioned in books on London Transport and deserves research.

The question of devoting a financial surplus to relief of rates deserves further study. There were several early attempts to remove tramways' obligation to relieve rates: the Dundee Act of 1898 did so, and an attempt was made in the Rochdale Act of 1900, but this was amended to apply only to lines outside the borough boundary (Garcke, 1901).

Then there is the question of comparisons with the rest of Great Britain. Nationally, tramways reached their peak in 1927 measured in passenger journeys and revenue, though maximum number of cars was in 1926 and the maximum route mileage was in 1923. But decline had already begun, and towns as large as Mansfield, Burton on Trent, Wigan and Rochdale had said farewell to their trams before London Transport took over in the capital.

Enthusiasts have tended to look for a variety of reasons for tramway abandonment, and many were used in public debate. But the professionals were largely clear that the reasons were financial and Hennessy makes the point that just as finance caused trams decline, so changed financial conditions could bring their revival (Hennessy, 1972). The financial problem was there in 1933; LPTB created the institutional framework to solve it, and London United's trolleybuses provided the practical means to do so.

Frank Pick has sometimes been identified as the moving spirit, in London's tramway abandonment. He was involved in the MET's renewal of lease negotiations and the decision to build the Feltham cars, but he had also been present at the launch of LUT's trolleybuses and knew the financial returns that C J Spencer quoted. He would also have been aware that as long ago as 1923, R Stuart Pilcher, the Edinburgh tramways manager, had said that an engineer was justified in replacing old plant by new if he could effect such annual economies as would meet charges on the displaced plant and the new plant, and show a commercial profit (Pilcher, 1923). Pilcher was then considering the Edinburgh conversion from cable to electric tramways, and although he ingeniously re-used much material, it gave him an unrivalled experience in writing off large amounts of modern capital. He later put it to further use in the Manchester conversion from electric trams to buses.

The sheer scale of London's tramways meant that their replacement would take at least a decade. So some improvements were made, partly by rehabilitating some of the LCC E1 Class cars (which could be done out of the revenue account) and also by including an item of tramway capital works in the 1934 LPTB bill which provided for the first trolleybus conversions. This was to convert the section from Aldgate to Grove Road from conduit to overhead, part of a larger scheme which the LCC had had in mind. Some light is thrown on this by Christian Barman, Pick's biographer who records that Pick was anxious to make the trolleybus overhead equipment as aesthetically acceptable as possible, knowing that it would have to be erected on inner-London ex-conduit routes.

Barman records that he asked the Ministry of Transport to call a conference of interested authorities to co-ordinate street furniture design, and suggested the Bow Road conduit to overhead conversion as a pilot project (Barman, 1979). Could it be that Pick, aware of the shortcomings of trolleybus overhead equipment, wanted to get approval with an installation of the less-intrusive tramway equipment, to pave the way for poles and twin wires in Bedford Square and Grays Inn Road?

The Ministry of Transport showed little enthusiasm, the conference never took place, and neither did the Bow Road conversion. And Pick did run into trouble with the aesthetics of trolleybus overhead!

Figure 2.9 LCC Tramways: Profitability and Debt Redemption, 1900-1928
a) Uses/Sources of Profits/Losses

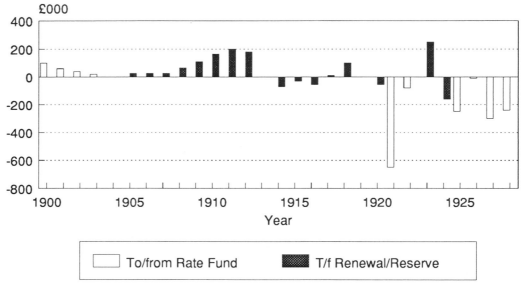

Profits transferred to and losses made
up from rates, renewals or reserve funds

b) Redemption of Debt
Effects on Outstanding Balances
of Profits and Transfers from Rates

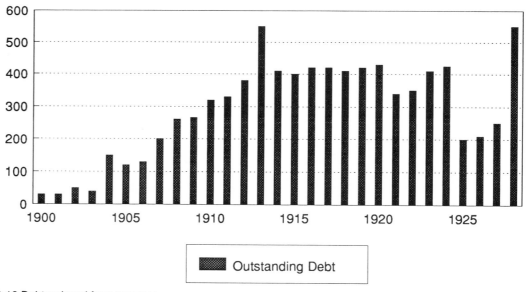

1913-16 Debt reduced from reserves;
1921-2, 1925-8 from rate fund transfers

Conclusions

From all the foregoing I conclude that the reasons for abandonment of London's tramways were primarily financial. An element in this was the exclusion of trams from the City and the West End, which encouraged bus development and later competition. The institutional framework prevented the tramway undertakings from responding adequately, and external controls were applied which paved the way for the unified London Transport.

But the first and most serious problems were extended loan repayments unmatched by life of assets, coupled with operating profits devoted to relief of rates rather than set aside as reserves or renewal funds. The huge sums demanded by local authorities from the London United company for street works were the equivalent of relief of rates, and contributed largely to its over-capitalisation. There were echoes of some of these problems in the Transport Act 1985, which converted local authority bus undertakings from municipal trading departments to 'arms-length' municipally-owned companies. These were revalued on a 'no profit, no loss' basis curiously reminiscent of the 1933 LPTB takeover. But already, bus operators' accounting had become progressively simpler, with buses bought increasingly out of revenue and less with loans (Groves, 1987). And there are continuing moves towards 'off-balance-sheet accounting' - with leased vehicles and services such as workshops, parts stores and even accounting and legal services 'bought-in' from specialist companies.

Having said all this, I am aware of the shortcomings of my own, all-too-brief researches. There are discrepancies in figures, for compensation to local authorities in 1933 for instance, which I have not had time to resolve between different sources. And there is scope for more and deeper analysis of accounts and accounting policies than I have attempted, and greater use of primary sources. So my second conclusion is the need for more research. There is scope for at least half-a-dozen PhD theses here, concentrating on the capital, rather than revenue, side.

My third conclusion is for the light railway and tramway projects of the future. Projects which are excellent in engineering, operation and contribution to the quality of life can be destroyed by financial foundations which are either excessive or out of step with replacement cycles.

My fourth conclusion is that there is scope for research into the value of the remaining tramway assets, a total of 35 depots and other buildings, plus the travelling habits built up - one hesitates to say goodwill - along the majority of tramway routes that are still bus-served. And perhaps the most tangible, yet self-effacing asset of all, the 500 miles of tramway power feeder conduits under London's pavements, currently being rented out to Mercury for its telecommunications network. The fact that nobody was prepared to name a value for this suggests to me that its value is considerable. Perhaps for the first time in 50 years, a conduit system is paying a handsome dividend.

Figure 2.10   Weekly Wage Rates
Tram and Bus Drivers/Conductors

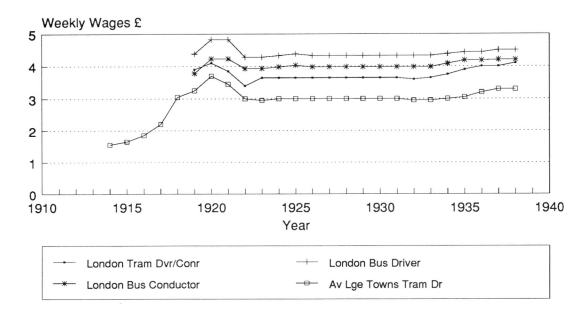

Source: Munby Tables B5.1, C5.8
Average Lge Towns: 52 large towns
to 1930, then 39 large towns.

References to Chapter 2

Allcock, John. Article in *Tramway and Railway World*, 1908

Baddeley, G E et al ('Southmet'). *The Tramways of Croydon*. Light Railway Transport League, 1960

Barker, T C and R M Robbins. *A History of London Transport, Volume II, The Twentieth Century to 1970*. London, George Allen & Unwin, 1974

Barman, Christian. *The Man Who Built London Transport: A Biography of Frank Pick*. Newton Abbott, David & Charles, 1979

Bett, W H and J C Gillham. *Great British Tramway Networks*. Light Railway Transport League, 1940

Bond, A W. *The British Tram, History's Orphan*. Gratwicke Lecture, Tramway and Light Railway Society/Tramway Museum Society, 1979

Dunbar, Charles S. *Idealism and Competition: The Fares Policy of the London County Council Tramways*. Paper to the Transport Ticket Society, 1967

Garcke, E. *Manual of Electrical Undertakings, 1900-1901*. London, Electrical Press

Garcke, E. *Manual of Electrical Undertakings, 1933-1934*. London, Electrical Press

Green, Oliver and John Reed. *The London Transport Golden Jubilee Book, 1933-1983*. London, Daily Telegraph, 1983

Harrison, Michael. *Consumables Price Index 1800 to 1954*. Personal communication, 1987

Hennessy, R S. *The Electrical Revolution (a study of the power supply industry)*. Newcastle-upon-Tyne, Oriel Press, 1972

Horne, J B and T B Maund. *Liverpool Transport, Volume 2*. Transport Publishing Company/Light Rail Transit Association, 1982

Jack, Douglas. *The Leyland Bus*. Glossop, Transport Publishing Company, 2nd Edition, 1984

Jackson, W E. *Achievement: A Short History of the History of the London County Council*. Longman, Green & Co., 1965

'Kennington'. *London County Council Tramways Handbook*. Tramway and Light Railway Society. 3rd Edition, 1977

Kitchen, A E. 'Simplification of Municipal Accounts', in *Bus and Coach*, January 1938

Kitchen, L D. 'London Transport After Six Years', in *Bus and Coach*, December, 1939

Klapper, C F. *The Golden Age of Buses*. Routledge, Kegan and Paul, 1978, for citation of Heavy Motor Car (Amendment Order), 1928 and subsequent legislation

London County Council. *Tramway Accounts, Historical Sumary*, 1928

London Passenger Transport Board Press Cuttings, *Book of Arbitration Proceedings, 1933-1935*. In National Tramway Archives, Crich

Marsh, S N B. *Tramways Department*. Pitmans Municipal Series, 1923

Munby, D L. *Inland Transport Statistics Great Britain 1900-1970*. Oxford, Clarendon Press, 1978

National Bus Company *Annual Report & Accounts 1978 and 1979*. NBC, 1979, 1980.
Lord Shepherd, Chairman, in his statement to the press, described the process of repayment as 'onerous' (23 May 1979) and on 18 June 1980 said that the process cost £811 per vehicle per year.

Pick, Frank. 'The London Passenger Transport Board, 1933-1938'. In *Bus & Coach*, May 1939

Pilcher, R Stuart. In *Tramway & Railway World*, 20 September, 1923

Pilcher, R Stuart. 'Bus, Tram, or Trackless Trolley'. In *Bus & Coach*, March 1930

Pilcher, R Stuart. 'Likely Effects of War on Transport Costs'. Paper for *Municipal Passenger Transport Association Conference, 1940*. (Conference cancelled) National Tramway Archives, Crich

'Rodinglea'. *Tramways of East London*. Tramway & Light Railway Society/ Light Railway Transport League, 1967

Silvers, Owen.'Why We Scrapped Our Trams'. In *Bus & Coach*, February 1929

Sleeman, J F. *The Rise and Decline of Municipal Transport*. Undated.

Smeeton, C S. *Metropolitan Electric Tramways*. Light Rail Transit Association. Vol I, 1984, Vol II, 1986

Townsin, A A. *Blue Triangle: AEC Buses*. Transport Publishing Company, 1980

Tramway & Railway World. Editorial: 'The Financial Crisis'. 20 March, 1920

Transport, Ministry of, Tramway Charges Advisory Committee. *Enquiry into LCC Tramways Fares Application, 1920*

Wilson, Geoffrey. *London United Tramways*. George, Allen & Unwin, 1971

Acknowledgements to Chapter 2

I would also like to acknowledge much help given by the archives staff at the National Tramway Museum, Crich, Reed Business Publishing Ltd. for the use of the archives of *Bus and Coach*, the Librarian of the Chartered Institute of Transport, the Bus and Coach Council for access to its archives, and Alan M Armour, formerly with Westinghouse, GEC and AEI, for information about electrical manufacturing and power supply. Much help was given by A Winston Bond, whose 1979 Gratwicke Lecture provided many important pointers for research, Bernard Acton, formerly chief management accountant, Trafford Metropolitan Borough, Tony Depledge, Managing Director, Blackpool Borough Transport, Philip Groves, formerly General Manager, Nottingham City Transport, June Beedham, formerly Press Officer, London Buses Ltd., Charles S Dunbar, author of *Idealism and Competition*, Oliver Green, formerly Curator, London Transport Museum, Lynne MacDiarmid for typing the manuscript, and lastly Martin Higginson for giving me the opportunity to open up what I hope will be a continuing exploration by many people of a complex and fascinating area of study.

3 LONDON TRAMWAY TECHNOLOGY

J H Price

Introduction

Sixty years ago, in 1927, nearly every large city in the developed world relied to some extent for its local transport on electric tramways. In North America alone there were nearly 400 systems (city and suburban), whereas today there are only about 300 in the entire world. However, most of this reduction in their number occurred between about 1935 and 1968. In the last 15 years the remaining tramways have shown a high degree of 'staying power'; there have been few abandonments, and a number of completely new tramways have been or are being built. Examples include: Calgary and Edmonton in Canada; Buffalo, Portland, Sacramento, San Diego and San Jose in the USA; Utrecht in Holland; Nantes and Grenoble in France; Czestochowa in Poland; Constantza in Romania; Helwan in Egypt; and Tunis in Tunisia, with more to follow. For the moment I am leaving aside Tyne & Wear and the Docklands Light Railway.

Electric tramways are capital-intensive when compared with buses or trolleybuses, though much less costly than underground railways. Operation of urban transport systems is rarely profitable today, due to imbalance between peak and off-peak demands which leads to expensive equipment being used only for three or four hours per day. There is usually social pressure to operate at the lowest possible fares, and to provide transport 'at cost'. In these circumstances there is a natural tendency to use the cheapest form of transport that will do the job.

Tramways with their fixed installations are not the cheapest form of transport. They survive in certain cities and countries because they offer certain advantages which in some circumstances outweigh the disadvantage in costs. My aim in this paper is to try and define these characteristics, and then relate them to the situation in London, to try and identify the reason why these advantages were insufficient to secure the retention of tramways in London, or in some cases were not relevant to the situation in London. I shall deal with them in the following order:

   I)   Passenger Capacity

   II)   Automatic Steering

   III)   Coupled Car Operation

   IV)   Current Collection Systems

   V)   Track Costs and Track Layout

   VI)   Rolling Stock Development Potential

   VII)   Through Services and Boundaries

   VIII) Financial Implications

As this study proceeds it will become evident that there were various factors peculiar to London (or to Britain) the effect of which has been to place obstacles in the way of continued tramway operation. British tramways generally and the London tramways in particular were prevented for various institutional reasons from making proper use of the possibilities of rails, which are numbers I to III of the foregoing list, namely: (I) the ability to carry overloads; (II) automatic steering; and (III) the ability to operate in trains.

7. *From its opening in 1906 until reconstruction in 1929–31, the Kingsway Subway was restricted to single-deck trams. 'G' class cars 563 and 596 are seen on the northern ramp, which is still in situ forty years after the subway's closure.* Commercial postcard

8. *Interior of an LCC class E/1 tramcar as built. Longitudinal wooden-slatted seats and straps for a large complement of standing passengers may be seen.* LCC

I   Passenger Capacity

To examine this aspect let us first go back to the period immediately before the formation of the London Passenger Transport Board in 1933. In the Summer of 1933 Mr A D Murdoch, Manager of the Melbourne & Metropolitan Tramways Board (M&MTB) in Australia visited the London County Council Tramways. Mr Murdoch interviewed Mr T E Thomas, General Manager of the LCC Tramways, and a summary of this interview was included in his report to the M&MTB, from which I quote:

> 'Mr Thomas is of the opinion that there is still room for up-to-date tram services where the traffic warrants the cost. For heavy traffic and close headways, trams are still superior. For mass transportation, they had proved that there was no superior instrument to the tramway.'

The full report is reproduced as Chapter 4 of this volume.

At the period concerned the typical LCC tramcar had a seating capacity of 73 or 74 passengers, whereas the newest types of London motor bus then seated 56 or 60. This gave the tram about a 25 per cent capacity advantage over the motor bus. By 1936 this advantage had been eroded by the arrival of the 70-seat London trolleybus, and it would have disappeared entirely by 1962 with the adoption in many British cities of the 78-seat Leyland Atlantean bus.

However, this insistence on seating figures as the measure of capacity is a peculiarly English phenomenon. In almost every other country of the world, a substantial proportion of passengers at peak times have to travel standing. This was less common in Britain, but by no means unknown and I will quote four examples:

1)   One evening in January 1946 I counted passengers boarding the single-deck trams of the Gateshead & District Tramways leaving Newcastle Central Station terminus in the evening rush hour for Low Fell, Bensham and Dunston. These cars seated 48 passengers on longitudinal wooden seats, leaving room for a double file of passengers to stand down the centre of the car, with passenger flow from rear entrance to front exit and a mobile conductor who worked from front to rear. The minimum load I counted was 76 and the maximum was 88, giving an overload of from 58 per cent to 83 per cent, and this was accepted as an everyday feature of travel on Tyneside. It helps to explain why Gateshead kept its trams and why they paid a steady 10 per cent dividend right up to the time they closed in 1951.

2)   The Wimbledon greyhound stadium in Plough Lane was served by a branch of the LCC Tramways from the No. 30 route in Garratt Lane. This route was replaced by trolleybuses in 1937 but the tram track was kept intact from Tooting Broadway to the greyhound stadium for use during race meetings. According to the late D R Pollock, these trams carried well over 100 passengers each, with two conductors (one on each deck) and with passengers standing on both decks and on the stairs. This continued for three years, 1937 - 1940, when circumstances changed because of the war. I have heard similar reports in regard to West Ham football ground, for which a small fleet of trams was kept specially at West Ham depot in 1938 - 1939 even after the normal service had been replaced by trolleybuses. In Newcastle on race days at Gosforth Park six Class F cars were capable of shifting 1,000 people.

3)   A few weeks ago I travelled on Britain's newest tramcar, Blackpool 644. The posted capacity was 52 seated and 16 standing, but by the time the car reached Talbot Square from Fleetwood it had 52 seated and 48 standing, an overload of 47 per cent.

4) In Glasgow, not only was a generous number of standing passengers allowed, but each tram carried the inscription 'There shall be no limit to the number of standing passengers carried on the last car on any route'. This inscription can still be seen on Glasgow tram 1282, at Crich.

This high overload capacity is a major advantage of a vehicle which uses steel rails, compared with vehicles on pneumatic tyres. It is referred to as crush capacity. I have to admit that the highest figure officially claimed anywhere in the world appears to be nine passengers to the square metre on the Peking articulated trolleybuses, which employ 'pushers' at the stops (Shanghai is thought to exceed this), but in Britain we associate crush capacity with peak hour travel on the London Underground. It is safe to let passengers crowd on to a rail vehicle until they fill the entire floor space available. No one forces them to do it; they pack themselves in, in order to travel quickly at the chosen time.

Standing in a rail vehicle is much more comfortable then standing in a rubber-tyred vehicle. Modern trams abroad usually have large standing lobbies with grab-rails, and a relatively small number of seats. In Warsaw, where three-car tram trains have to do the work of a Metro, each tram has only about 20 seats but can carry six times as many passengers standing.

Britain has always been an exception, due to our widespread use of double deck vehicles. From the 1850s and 1860s respectively it became common for horse-drawn buses and trams to have some seats on the roof. A high proportion of passengers therefore travelled sitting down. Electrification permitted larger and more powerful tramcars to be built on the same double-deck principle, initially with open top decks, later with enclosed tops.

Most provincial tramways made good use of their tramcars' overload capacity, for instance Bury trams were fitted with ceiling grab-rails upstairs, but those in London were subjected to a local Metropolitan Police ruling restricting the number of standing passengers to one-third of the seating capacity of the lower deck. This effectively threw away one of the tramcar's main advantages.

The three principal London tramway operators (LCC, MET, LUT) each had fleets of large bogie cars which in the period before 1914 gave them a substantial advantage over the motor bus, at that time typically a 34-seater. From the early 1920s this advantage was gradually eroded by the improvements in the motor bus.

On the West Croydon-Crystal Palace route a steep hill required the use of small trams with hand-operated track brakes; these were replaced by 60-seat trolleybuses in 1936.

Some tramways enlarged their curve clearances to allow the use of longer trams, eg the modern double deckers in Liverpool and Blackpool. This was prevented in London by the design of the LCC depots. The twin effect of high land values and the underground conduit system of current-collection combined to influence the design and layout of the depots, with access by a traverser (or transfer table). These traversers were designed for 35 feet cars, and to use longer cars would have meant rebuilding every depot and moving the roof supports. Only one LCC depot (Telford Avenue) was built with sufficient clearance for extra-long cars, and this was put to good use from 1937 onwards with the Feltham type cars. Even so, structural alterations had to be made at Charlton overhaul works to permit these extra-long tramcars to enter the buildings for their overhauls.

To sum up, we can say that the London tramways, and particularly the London County Council Tramways, did not make effective use of the advantage of rails in carrying heavy loads and that this was due to a combination of historical and legislative factors, some of which were peculiar to London.

9. *The Kingsway subway in 1952, shortly before closure. The smooth styling of the new RT type bus contrasts with the HR/2 class tram, over twenty years old, but still one of London's newest trams, on service 35 from Highgate (Archway Station) to Forest Hill.* J H Price

10. *Just three months before the outbreak of the second world war, which prolonged the existence of London's trams into the 1950s, class E/3 trams load on the Victoria Embankment on 19 May 1939. Route 26 ran from Clapham Junction and crossed the Thames twice, at Westminster Bridge and the back over Blackfriars Bridge to terminate at London Bridge (Borough). The 35 was a long route which took 85 minutes to travel from Forest Hill to Highgate (Archway Station) via the Kingsway Subway. The loading island separating the tramway reservation from the roadway is clearly too narrow to cope with the numbers of passengers boarding and alighting here.* London Transport Museum U29770

II   Automatic Steering

This advantage of rail vehicles takes two main forms, viz.

  i)   the ability to operate at normal speed in a confined space, and
  ii)   the ability to operate in trains

Let us deal first with the former advantage.

The ability to operate at normal speed in a confined space, with the rails providing automatic steering, means that trams can operate through tunnels or on viaducts and that these structures can be built to the minimum dimensions. They can also run along narrow strips of land separated from roads and use these without interference from other road users.

The principal example in London was the Kingsway Tram Subway between Bloomsbury and the Victoria Embankment, built in 1905 - 1908 as part of a slum-clearance and redevelopment scheme. It created a double-track tram tunnel from Southampton Row to the Victoria Embankment beneath Waterloo Bridge. A London County Council delegation had been to the USA and had reported favourably on the tramway subways which they had seen in Boston.

Due to the presence of a large sewer under Holborn, the subway was originally built to dimensions that would only admit single-deck cars. This prevented the integration of the subway services with the rest of the LCC network, and 20 years later the LCC decided to reconstruct it to admit double-deck cars. During the reconstruction in 1930 temporary bus services were run on adjacent streets but attracted fewer passengers than the trams, and were reduced.

The enlarged subway was opened in January 1931, with a new pattern of through services between north and south London. These were a great success and in their first full year attracted an extra 300,000 passengers. The 1933 Melbourne visitor was told that the extra revenue obtained fully justified the expenditure on enlarging the subway.

It was unfortunate that there was a change of political control on the LCC in 1907, when the Progressive party was defeated by the Municipal Reformers (Conservatives), who were critical of the large amounts of money spent on the tramways for what they considered to be an insufficient financial return. The LCC had been considering building further tramway subways to give north-south connections across central London, including one that would have run beneath St. Paul's Churchyard, but none were built, in this case because of the opposition of the Corporation of the City of London. This lack of connections across central London played into the hands of the bus operators, whose services penetrated the centre of London.

The LCC also had plans for additional surface tramways in central London. When the new Lambeth Bridge was designed, the girders were specified as to be capable of carrying a tramway; this would have run to Victoria. The LCC also had a plan for a surface tramway from Blackfriars Bridge across Ludgate Circus to Farringdon Road terminus. This had been proposed in a 1919 Bill but rejected. It was revived in 1924 in the form of a single line for use only at night, for rolling stock transfers, but was rejected, and Mr T E Thomas told the 1933 Melbourne delegate that he hoped the new Transport Board would be able to overcome the opposition of the city Corporation. Unfortunately it soon became clear that the new London Passenger Transport Board had no such intention.

The Kingsway Subway trams took only six minutes between Westminster and Bloomsbury, and were able to run at full speed on the side-of-the-road Victoria Embankment track and in the Kingsway tunnel. When Parliament was sitting late, Members of Parliament from constituencies remote from London often used the various Bloomsbury hotels and reached them from Westminster by the late-night trams.

11. *The laying of tramway street track is a spectacular process, the more so when conduit track is involved. The similarity between this 1929 scene at Gardiner's Corner, Aldgate and that some sixty years later at Piccadilly Gardens, Manchester is remarkable (see photograph in Railway Gazette International, November 1991, page 766).* LCC

12. *Relaying a crossover at the complex Whitechapel High Street, Commercial Road, Commercial Street, Leman Street intersection in the East End. The depth to which the road had to be excavated to accommodate the conduit yokes (one of which is seen lower right) made tracklaying a tedious and expensive task.*
London Transport Museum 25131

When the subway trams were replaced in 1952 by buses running on the surface the running time was substantially increased. Many users found other ways to travel and traffic dropped. In 1964 part of the tunnel was reopened as a road underpass for traffic from Waterloo Bridge to Kingsway. The 20 feet wide subway which had accommodated two lines of tramway traffic could only accept a single file of steerable road vehicles, and had to be fitted with expensive ventilation equipment to deal with motor exhaust fumes. Electric traction requires no ventilation plant and the cars or trains themselves promote the circulation of air.

The Kingsway Subway was expensive to construct, partly because of the very high standards imposed by the LCC. All LCC tramway construction was extremely solid and enduring. The concrete in the subway was so hard that it wasn't worth trying to dig out the tram track, and it is still there today, under the roadway. The subway roof girders in Lancaster Place were found to be in such good condition after 50 years that they were simply lowered on to new pillars to form the supports for the road ramp. Another example of solid and enduring LCC work is that the tramway power supply cable ducts under the streets are still in use today for commercial telecommunication purposes. After the trams finished, London Transport leased them to Rediffusion; their present-day successors are Mercury.

It is a pity that none of the other tramway subways envisaged by the LCC ever materialised. There are several examples abroad where the existence of a subway or tunnel has been the main factor in keeping a tramway system; examples are Boston, Newark, Pittsburgh, Philadelphia and Marseille. Many other tram subways have been built in the last 30 years, such as San Francisco, Vienna, Antwerp, Cologne, Brussels, Dortmund, Hanover, Bielefeld, Düsseldorf, Essen, Stuttgart and short sections elsewhere. The Tyne & Wear Metro tunnels under Newcastle and Gateshead play the same role as modern continental tram tunnels. The presence of tramway subways in the central part of a city also encourages other provision of special tracks in the suburbs.

Having described what the London tramways did to take advantage of automatic steering, we must now consider what they failed to do. Many British provincial tramways included tramway reservations along the centre strip of dual-carriage roads. The Ministry of Transport in its handbook *Design and Layout of Roads in Built-Up Areas* recommended providing a 20 feet strip along the centre of any suburban road which might be the subject of tramway extension. The first city to adopt this form of construction on a large scale was Liverpool, whose city engineer J A Brodie claimed that this reduced the cost of tramway construction by about one-third.

London had no median-strip reserved track tramways, not even along the very wide Westhorne Avenue in Eltham, but 20 feet strips were in fact provided along the main roads of the LCC housing estates at Becontree and St Helier. Becontree with 120,000 inhabitants was the largest municipal housing estate in the world and would certainly have justified the installation of tramways. St Helier had 40,000 inhabitants and the LCC had tried to persuade the South Metropolitan Tramways to extend from Mitcham Cricket Green to St Helier. The difficulty in both cases was that these estates were beyond the limits of the LCC's own boundaries and tramway operating area.

The Middlesex County Council actively considered this form of construction for the Uxbridge Road between Southall and Hayes. The moving spirit was probably County Councillor W B Pinching, an electrical engineer, who had led a delegation to Birmingham to see the new reserved track along the Bristol Road. The uncertainty about the formation of the new transport board meant that no action was taken.

It would have been difficult to provide very much reserved track in inner London, save eventually in pedestrian shopping areas, but many possibilities existed further out, and some of these lines would have acted as feeders to the railways, with substantial rush-hour traffic. London might well have developed a tramway route pattern similar to that in Moscow, where the tram routes in the inner areas have closed but new routes have been and are still being built in the suburbs. The same depots which were once near the outer terminal are now near the inner terminal. Absence of dedicated high-capacity short-distance surface feeders to the Underground is still a weakness of London's transport system.

13. *Installing the one-way track system at Vauxhall Cross, early in 1938. By this date, heavy motor traffic is evident.* LPTB (Topical Press). London Transport Museum 25129

If London had used high-capacity single-deck trams instead of double-deckers there would possibly have been some scope for diverting the trams along sections of little-used railway lines, very much as is now being done for the Docklands Light Railway and is being considered for Croydon. The nearly universal use of double-deck cars on London's tramways meant that this possibility was never seriously examined. In the days of privately-owned railway companies it would also have been subject to administrative difficulties.

Automatic steering can be useful in a variety of special cases, such as short lengths of tunnel or bridgework at major traffic intersections, in pedestrian shopping precincts, or in narrow three-lane roads with a contra-flow tram track against the kerb, as in St Etienne. The principle is the same as that of the contra-flow bus lane, but it works best with trams. Trams can operate safely at low speed through pedestrian precincts because you know precisely where they are going and where they are not going.

For any of these improvements to take place it is necessary that the tramways have a secure future, otherwise the investment would be lost. If the future of the tramways is in doubt, then they become subject to the dictum 'He who hesitates is lost'.

Another advantage of automatic steering on private tracks is that these tracks can be fenced in and thus rendered suitable for higher speeds. Liverpool Corporation obtained a general speed limit of 30 mph on its reserved tracks (enclosed by hedges) whereas the highest London tram speed limits were 20 mph on the Metropolitan Electric Tramways and London United, but only 16 mph on the LCC Tramways. This LCC limit was later increased to an overall 20 mph with a few sections at 25 mph. Buses on pneumatic tyres at this period were allowed 30 mph. Trams with their multiple braking systems can run safely at any speed likely to be permitted for buses, but in London the Ministry of Transport and the Metropolitan Police did not accept this reasoning.

The fastest London tram services were MET route 40 from Cricklewood to North Finchley, and LCC route 11 from Highgate Village to Moorgate. In 1931 MET route 40 was the fastest scheduled urban tram service in Europe. Even in 1950, London trams were still faster than some of those elsewhere in Britain, mainly because of quicker deceleration at stops.

One further advantage of automatic steering is the ability to operate safely in fog, but this is less important now than in the past due to the run-down in 'smokestack' industries. I well remember a winter evening in 1943 when the bus service from Lewisham to the Crystal Palace had ceased entirely due to fog, while the trams from Lewisham to Dulwich were still running, and took me most of the way home.

III Coupled Car Operation

The most useful feature of railed transport is the ability to operate vehicles in trains. This is the key factor in the survival of many European tramways. In London the advantage was thrown away in an attempt to reply to unrestricted motor bus competition.

Following the precedent set by the steam tramways, several British tramways that were electrified in the 1890s began by using motor and trailer cars, eg Leeds, Hull, Coventry, Liverpool and Guernsey, but the Board of Trade insisted that a brakesman should always be present on the trailer, and this removed much of the financial advantage. Furthermore, the large British double-decker could be considered as the equivalent in seating capacity of the Continental car and trailer.

Because it could use only single-deck cars on its Kingsway Subway routes, the LCC Tramways considered the possible use of coupled single-deck motor trams on these services. The Metropolitan Police were hostile, but the Board of Trade agreed to an experiment. Subway single-deckers 572 and 573 were fitted up in 1910 as a twin unit and tried on the Euston-Hampstead route during 1911. The equipment used was particularly complicated, since the LCC's underground conduit system of current supply, with occasional changes of polarity between adjacent electrical sections, meant that the cars could not be coupled electrically in the way familiar on electric trains. Each car had to draw its own

14. *The construction of a gyratory system south of Westminster Bridge in 1950, part of the traffic arrangements for the following year's Festival of Britain, brought the laying of London's last new conduit tram track. Class E/1 tram no.1823 negotiates the working site, en route for Wesminster.* J H Meredith

15. *This illustration of conduit track under construction at the Festival of Britain diversion shows the massive cross section of the supporting yokes and depth of foundations needed for the conduit system.* J H Meredith

traction current separately from the supply rails, the rear car's controller being actuated electromagnetically from the front car. There were several accidents during the trials and permission to operate over a longer trial period was refused. It was a very clumsy control system, but the use of the underground conduit system of supply made that unavoidable. The only alternative at that time would probably had been the use of compressed-air operated control servomotors as on the St. Gervais to Vallorcine railway in France, which would have been even more complicated.

The experiment therefore failed for technical reasons peculiar to the London conduit collection system. It would have worked far better with an overhead supply, which would not have the interruptions in supply necessary at conduit points and crossings. An experiment on these lines was later carried out by the Metropolitan Electric Tramways.

The LCC Tramways next sought permission to operate trailers, and in order to overcome the objections of the Metropolitan Police they obtained the sanction of Parliament in the London County Council (Tramways and Improvements) Act 1912. These powers applied to most of the South London system, and 158 open top double-deck trailers were placed in service. They helped the LCC Tramways handle very heavy wartime and peak-hour traffic, and in 1921 the LCC claimed that the one-hour peak service along the Victoria Embankment comprised 195 cars and 27 trailers. In 1922 they decided to build a new trailer depot at Brixton Hill.

Despite successful operation, the LCC Tramways gave up the use of trailers in stages during 1922 - 1924. The local council would not allow them to run in Wimbledon and this led to their withdrawal from the Tooting route, despite the adoption of 60 hp motors on new cars designed to haul trailers. Increasing competition from improved types of motor bus led to a decision by the Council to speed up the tram service by withdrawing the trailers on the other routes. An incidental advantage was that since all LCC motor trams now had top covers, they could use the publicity slogan 'Under Cover All the Way', which referred to the use of open tops on the buses.

The greatest single factor in the survival of tramways on the Continent has been the introduction of the articulated tramcar, coupled with fare and ticket systems which enable such cars to be operated by one man. The articulated car can be regarded as two or three cars coupled and joined by vestibule connections. Although an articulated car can cost as much as three buses, it carries three times the load and yet requires only one operator. It is this advantage that has kept the Continent's tramways in being, and several German towns that were considering tramway abandonment changed their minds and adopted articulated cars, examples being Krefeld, Würzburg and Mainz.

Would Londoners have accepted single-deck vehicles with a large standing load and fewer seats? We can find the answer by observing whether they take to the Docklands Light Railway. However, I doubt whether they would have accepted this form of travel for, say, a slow one-hour journey from Westminster to Thornton Heath Pond.

In my view the introduction of articulated cars on the existing London tramways would not have ensured their survival, but if they had been used on segregated tracks offering faster running than alternative road vehicles, they might well have succeeded.

One reason for the possible unpopularity of articulated cars in London might have been long headways. In 1952 the manager of the Hannover tramways told an LRTL party that 'Germany could not afford the luxury of running single cars'. Long headways are traditional there (15 or 20 minutes), but the timetable is usually displayed at every stop and adhered to, so that you know exactly how long you have to wait.

An ancillary factor in London was the prevalence of the stub-end termini where the cars had to reverse. Most articulated trams of the 1960s and early 1970s were built as single-enders with fixed seating and no offside doors, thus allowing more space for seating. In London the stub termini might have required the use of double-ended articulated cars with either longitudinal seating, back-to-back seats, or reversible seats, all of which are less comfortable than modern bus seats.

16. *Class HR/2 car 1877 negotiates new trackwork at the southern end of Westminster Bridge in 1950 as an RT-type bus passes on route 12. By this date one or two unconventional members of the gang of workmen are hatless.*   London Transport Museum H/16610

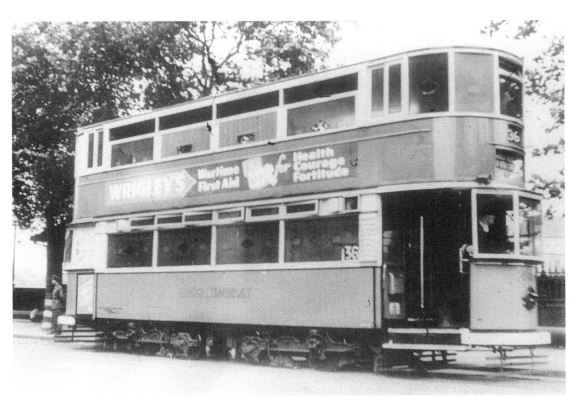

17. *The Embankment roadside reservation in London Transport days; car no.1506 on service 36 (Abbey Wood–Victoria Embankment via Blackfriars Bridge). In tramway days, Victoria Embankment was served by up to a dozen routes; now the former tramway reservation is buried under an all-purpose dual carriage-way road and sees only a restricted peak-hour bus service on a single route.*   D Conrad

IV Current Collection Systems

Trams throughout the world today use the overhead system of current collection, usually at 550 or 600 volts direct current. These are the highest voltages considered acceptable for use in public thoroughfares. The overhead system of current collection is normally used with sliding current collectors which cannot leave the wire or take the wrong turning at junctions.

The LCC used an unusual system of current collection, the Underground Conduit. This came about because Parliament gave the London boroughs a power of veto over the use of overhead wires in their streets. Most of them exercised this veto, forcing the LCC to use a system copied from New York in which power was fed to the cars through positive and negative conductor rails enclosed in a subterranean tube between the rails. This tube had a three quarters of an inch slot in the top through which a plough suspended from the under-side of the car picked up the current by means of two spring-loaded collector shoes.

This complication was quite unnecessary in most of London and was an example of legislative folly. There were only three places in London where the conduit system showed any advantage, namely:

1) The environs of Greenwich Observatory, where an insulated return system was specified to avoid electrical interference with the scientific instruments;

2) The Kingsway Subway, in which the use of conduit current collection reduced the dimensions and therefore the cost of the tunnel;

3) Westminster Bridge and the adjacent portion of the Victoria Embankment which included some of the most famous vistas in the world and where Parliament itself would probably have disallowed overhead wires.

There was no reason why overhead collection should not have been allowed in the other boroughs such as Lambeth, Wandsworth, Lewisham, Stepney and Hackney. All their streets had two lines of poles for the street lighting, and single overhead wires are not very noticeable. In Croydon, the tram wires were not taken down until several weeks after the trams ceased to run in April 1951, and the *Croydon Advertiser* carried out a public survey one Saturday in North End, a busy shopping street, asking pedestrians what was different in the street compared with the previous week. Only three persons out of about forty interviewed even noticed that the tram wires had been taken down since the previous week.

In North London, when the time came in 1937 - 1939 to abandon the conduit tramways and install a trolleybus system with poles and wires, the earlier objections to overhead wires were conveniently forgotten.

The London County Council in most of the inner London boroughs was therefore saddled with a system that cost about two and a half times as much to install as an overhead-wire tramway, and increased the cost of both track and car maintenance. The weakest point was the plough collector. These had a very short life and the LCC had to maintain a huge stock of spare ploughs.

London kept the conduit system until final closure in 1952. It was not the last conduit tramway in the world, being survived by Bordeaux to 1953 and Washington DC to 1963. In the last years of the South London tramways, the financial loss on working was substantially equal to the extra cost of conduit operation. At that time most of Britain's major provincial tramways were still operating at a profit, whereas the London tramways according to London Transport's 1950 Report produced an annual deficit of £1.25 million.

There was however one advantage with the conduit system. The original construction, with 400 lb. cast iron yokes set in concrete, was extremely solid and enduring. The LCC and LPTB never had any trouble with their track foundations. All they had to do was replace the running rails and T-rails as they wore out, and weld up the worn points and crossings.

After the first few years, the LCC tried to find cheaper alternatives to the conduit system. First they tried the Griffiths-Bedell surface contact system along the Bow Road, with a magnet under the car that would attract to itself a metal stud which in rising from its socket would make a circuit with the traction supply. It was a complete failure, and led to an expensive lawsuit between the LCC and the manufacturers and patentees. It was also a factor in the 1907 LCC election when the Progressives were ousted by the Municipal Reformers.

Eventually, some of the outer boroughs agreed to overhead wires, and these were used from 1908 onward in Woolwich, West Norwood, Eltham, Downham, Victoria Park and Amhurst Park. Cars for these routes and those working through on to other operators' lines had to be dual fitted for conduit and overhead collection, but many North London cars ended their days without ever being fitted with trolley poles, and the same applied to cars 101 - 160, bought as late as 1931.

In the case of the Woolwich to Eltham route, the Royal Observatory at Greenwich insisted on an all-insulated system with both positive and negative overhead wires. This subsisted until the observatory moved to Hurstmonceaux Castle in Sussex in the 1920s as a result of the forthcoming electrification of the North Kent lines of the Southern Railway.

Early in 1933, the LCC Tramways carried out some experiments with bow and pantograph collectors on the line between Downham and Grove Park, using E/1 type cars. Little has been published about the reason for these trials, but thanks to the report of the 1933 visitor from the Melbourne and Metropolitan Tramways Board, who held discussions with the general manager of the LCC Tramways, Mr T E Thomas, and his departmental heads, we now know that the LCC Tramways were definitely considering a change to overhead current collection on at least some of the parts of their system. The evidence for this is twofold:

   1)   Mr Thomas told the Melbourne Tramways Manager that the operating expenses for the conduit lines were about £140,000 per year (or £1160 per mile) more than for the overhead system, and said 'they would be glad to get rid of this incubus, and, when the day arrives for renewals, it is possible that under the new authority there will be some effort to do so'.

   2)   London Transport's 1934 Act gave the Board powers to convert from conduit to overhead the line from Aldgate to Bow Bridge. Bow Road was wide and straight and well suited for tramways - in recent years it was proposed that a part of the Docklands Light Railway should run along it.

Neither of these schemes materialised, and in the event only one short section of the London tramways was ever converted from conduit to overhead, and that only for the last few months of operation prior to replacement by trolleybuses. This was the line along Egerton Road from Stamford Hill change pit to Stamford Hill depot, while the depot was being altered to admit trolleybuses.

Conversion to overhead supply would have had to be phased in over several years, if only to spread the cost. In Liverpool a decision was taken in about 1936 to alter the overhead line to accept sliding collectors, but by 1945 only half the mileage had been converted, and no cars were equipped.

A secondary effect of the conduit system was that it was extremely expensive to alter the layout, and this was a deterrent to carrying out road improvements. An example was the Streatham High Road, where the road was widened in the late 1930s but the tram track was never realigned. Several proposed one-way road systems, for example at New Cross, were not implemented until after the tramways had closed in 1952. This postponement was a consequence of the decision to abandon the tramways, and the resulting wish to avoid spending money on something with a short life. The only post-war improvement in the track layout of the London tramways was the Westminster Bridge Road twin roundabout of 1950, paid for by the government as part of the cost of the Festival of Britain.

On overhead-wire tramways abroad, it is quite common to make changes to the layout - even temporary changes - in conjunction with road works. Each tramway has a permanent way yard with a

18. *Tramway track maintenance gang at work on a conduit track junction on a wet night.*

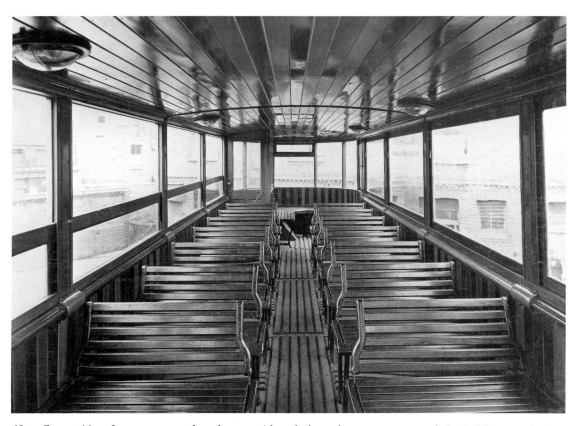

19. *Competition from more modern buses, with upholstered seats, encouraged the LCC to modernise many of its trams. This view shows the upper deck of a class E car with the slatted wooden seats with which most of London's older trams were built. Photographed on 31 May 1907.*

good stock of rails, points and crossings. Glasgow Corporation were able to install new crossovers in a weekend, limiting the interruption to tram traffic to the night hours. That could not have been done on the conduit system.

V Track Costs and Track Layouts

Logic suggests that laying a double track railway, with all the load carried on four thin strips of steel, should cost no more, and perhaps less, than building a complete roadway of sufficient capacity to carry the same volume of traffic, with foundations to match.

Tramways operated with single-deck cars or trains, such as articulated cars, can use open trackwork made up from standard railway components. A good example is the Tyne & Wear Metro, which is not a tramway trying to behave like a railway, it is a railway trying to behave like a tramway.

This however assumes that the track is unpaved. In Britain, most tramways were laid in the street, and Parliament insisted that the tramway operator should pave and maintain the road surface between the rails and for 18 inches on either side. This dated from the days when the horses pulling the tram could be said to wear out the road, but it was never repealed, despite a serious attempt to do so in 1951. Most conduit track was paved in stone setts, because the alternative wood block paving used in Central London would swell in wet weather and pinch the conduit slot.

The almost universal use in Britain of double-deck tramcars had the effect of increasing both the construction cost and the maintenance cost of the track. The extra weight of the upper deck and its passengers increased the axle-loading, thus a typical four-wheel car would weigh about 12 tons (6 tons per axle), a London-type maximum traction bogie car weighed about 16.5 tons, distributed say 6 tons on each motored axle and 2.25 tons on each pony axle, and the London Feltham type trams weighed about 18.5 tons and probably had the heaviest axle load in Britain on their driving axles.

The axle loading determined the hammer-blow on the rail joints, which would wear out more quickly than the rest of the rail, leading to premature replacement or the cropping of rail ends and moving-up of rails. The correct solution was the use of welded rail joints, but this meant more night work at overtime rates of pay.

In Britain, the Board of Trade would not allow double-deck cars to carry passengers on open railway-type trackwork without check rail. All such tramways therefore had to be laid with grooved rail, which is much more expensive than bullhead or Vignoles rail. The only exception was the Swansea & Mumbles line, which used double-deck cars with railway-profile wheels. These cars did not run on street track. If they were to run in the street they would have required a wide and deep groove, using rail known as dock rail, which would probably be unacceptable to other road users. Blackpool uses a compromise wheel-profile and obtained an exemption in 1971 allowing them to run double-deckers on their private tracks not fitted with check rail.

Operation of tramway profile wheels on open railway track is feasible if the track is laid precisely to gauge, without following the railway practice of widening the gauge on curves. A tram wheel has a shallow flange and a narrow tread, so on a curve laid wide-to-gauge it would fall inside. Liverpool Transport found this out when they moved some trams along railway track to a scrap merchant on the Kirkby Trading Estate and the cars kept derailing. Blackpool 147 when on test at Trolleyville USA at Olmsted Falls derailed 22 times in one day. To avoid this happening, the points and crossings would have to be of the solid raised-groove type, but could not then accept railway vehicles. This type of junction was first installed by the MET at Turnpike Lane in 1931.

So the use of double-deck cars with wheel profiles to fit British Standard grooved tramway rail would have prevented London trams from running on railway-type track even when, as in the Kingsway Subway, there was no need for the track to be paved. This prevented any thoughts of running trams along sections of existing little-used or disused railway, which in any case would not have been able to accept double-deck cars within the constraints of the railway loading gauge, as already mentioned.

20. *LCC's modernisation resulted in a new, red livery for the reseated E/1 cars in the late 1920s, as seen on No.1817 emerging from its depot to take up service on route 2 (Embankment–Wimbledon). The road sign warns pedestrians to "Beware of the cars crossing".*   LCC. London Transport Museum 25127

21. *Technical developments were also thoroughly tested. E/1 car no.1172, seen at Grove Park on route 52 (Grove Park to City via Old Kent Road) has been fitted with a pantograph in place of the usual trolley pole, for use on the overhead-wired Downham–Grove Park section of the route.*
LCC. London Transport Museum 25123

There are many examples on the Continent of single-deck trams running on track made up from standard railway components, and this track usually has a considerably longer life than tramway track laid in grooved rail, in addition to its lower first cost. On the Belgian Vicinal tramways, provided the joints were welded, the track was expected to last for 40 years.

VI   Rolling Stock Development Potential

The London tramways in the period immediately prior to the formation of the LPTB in 1933 were ahead of most British tramways in rolling stock design and equipment. This resulted from competition between buses and trams, which forced the London tramways to make improvements in their cars such as improved seating and lighting and higher running speeds, as compared to provincial cities where the municipal tramways were protected against competition. By 1932 all LCC trams had fully upholstered seats downstairs and cushioned or partly cushioned seats upstairs.

The London tramways were already ahead of most others in rolling stock design and equipment. The Metropolitan Electric Tramways were running the fastest urban tramway service in Europe, from Golders Green to North Finchley at an average of 12 mph with four stops per mile. Only two other British urban tramways ever equalled this, the Middlewood route at Sheffield and the Levenhall route at Edinburgh. Liverpool ran faster in the suburbs, but this was offset by slow running in the inner area.

The Metropolitan Electric Tramways were trying out some very promising ideas. These included bow collectors, trolley skids, passenger flow with front exits, air brakes, contactor control suitable for coupled cars, cross-field electric braking, weak field control, line-breakers, and monomotor bogies with each motor driving two axles. The best MET trams in 1933 were more advanced technically than almost any others in Europe, and were equalled only in North America. If tramway development had continued, London would no doubt have kept this lead.

The LCC Tramways were less adventurous than the MET, but had produced a prototype car, No 1, for the Kingsway Subway routes. The Melbourne Manager was told in 1933 that any future London trams would have equal-wheel bogies with 26.5 inch wheels, lightweight motors and helical gears. No orders had been placed for further cars, but in supplying parts for car No 1, Hurst Nelson & Co had made patterns and jigs for the headstocks and bolsters in readiness for series production.

It is possible that the general line of development that occurred in Liverpool between 1933 and 1937 represented what might have happened in London but for the change of policy.

In fact the forthcoming merger had held up several orders and projects. The Metropolitan Electric Tramways were apparently considering buying further Feltham type cars to equip route 59 (Holborn to Waltham Cross); they had extended the sidings at Edmonton Town Hall to take 40 feet long cars and had bought a strip of land for use in enlarging Edmonton Depot. The MET and Walthamstow Tramways were planning a new line from Tottenham to Walthamstow, the LCC Tramways were planning a line from Eltham to Grove Park, and the London United Tramways were planning track improvements on the Uxbridge route. A substantial proportion of the MET tracks were completely relaid in 1929 - 1933, as were the LUT tracks in Hounslow and from Ealing to Southall.

At first, London Transport continued this process and relaid much of the Highgate to North Finchley route in 1933 - 1934, and most of the Croydon track from Norbury to Purley in 1935 - 1936.

The LCC were conscious of the need to reduce tramway noise levels and adopted quiet-running helical gears and roller bearing axleboxes, with a radial arm instead of the horn blocks. These were in cars 101 - 159 which were probably the quietest trams in London, except for some gear-howl when worn.

In the 1940s new trams in Europe began to copy American technology, with hypoid gears, multi-notch acceleration and braking, and rubber-insert resilient wheels and gears. These features enable the tram to be considerably quieter than the bus, and it is impressive to see modern Continental articulated trams tiptoeing their way through city centres with no more than a 'whoosh'. This environmental

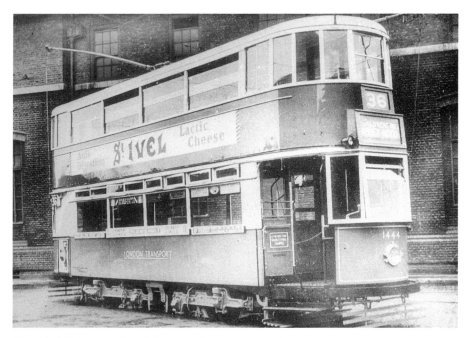

22. *A 1934 example of fleet modernisation. Rebuilt M/E3 car no.1444, seen in an official London Transport photograph at Charlton Works.* LPTB

23. *The company tramways were more radical than LCC and the suburban municipalities in fleet modernisation before the formation of London Transport. Metropolitan Electric Tramways no.330 is one of the three experimental 'Feltham' cars, which heralded the combined fleet of 100 such vehicles built in 1930–31 for MET and London United Tramways. A passenger is seen boarding at the rear of the 'front exit' car at Golders Green Underground Station on route 40 to North Finchley. Two 'T' type single deck buses may be seen in the bus station, which is still in use.* LPTB. London Transport Museum 25121

advantage has worked in the tram's favour and there are many cases in which environmental pressure groups have campaigned for tramway extension or retention in preference to buses, and for the adoption of trams in places where they have never previously run.

Londoners never had the chance to sample these very quiet trams, but there were some in Blackpool, and one in Leeds, No 602, which is now preserved in operating condition at Crich. When running in Leeds this car was nicknamed Pussyfoot, and it ran so quietly that on one occasion in Middleton Woods on route No 12 it surprised and killed a fox.

Eventually in the late 1970s the introduction of thyristor control by eliminating resistance losses gave the tram a substantial advantage in energy costs. The introduction of the silicon diode rectifier reduced conversion losses in power transmission and these two factors have together cut energy consumption by between 25 per cent and 30 per cent. These advantages also apply to the trolleybus and the electric train, and explain the resumption of large-scale railway electrification in Britain, the operation in South Yorkshire of an experimental trolleybus line and the proposal to reintroduce trolleybuses in Bradford on the routes to Wibsey and Buttershaw.

VII   Through Services and Boundaries

One unfortunate aspect of London's tramways was the way in which divided ownership hampered the introduction of through services between the separate operators' lines. I do not propose to dwell on this as it belongs entirely to history, but in several cases through services were not introduced until motor bus competition had taken hold (1912 - 1914). Between London and Croydon it did not begin until 1926, and between Croydon and Tooting it was left to London Transport to introduce through running in December 1933, with route 30.

A particularly unfortunate case was the lack of a connection between Tottenham and Walthamstow, proposed at intervals since 1902 but never built.

The London & Home Counties Traffic Advisory Committee of the Ministry of Transport tried to persuade the MET and LUT to introduce through running at Acton, but it failed through local opposition.

In some cases there were technical snags, such as the need to fit through running cars with both trolley poles and conduit collection. Through-running between Ilford and its neighbour tramways was ruled out by Ilford's use of different wheel profiles.

The benefits of through running were particularly marked on the Croydon route. When the Norbury to Purley service was operated wholly by Croydon Corporation, with four-wheel cars, the average speed was 7.5 miles per hour. When the service was taken over by LCC type E/1 bogie cars the speed was increased to 10.5 miles per hour and the number of passengers began to rise sharply. The LCC provided the cars while Croydon Corporation obtained delivery of 25 new E/1 type cars of their own.

VIII   Financial Implications

This aspect is being dealt with separately by Ian Yearsley, but I will include a brief note on the relationship between construction and operating costs and technology, including that of the motor bus.

The London Tramway operators were a mixture of successful and less successful ventures. The most successful were the London County Council and Ilford Council, followed by the Metropolitan Electric Tramways and West Ham Corporation. Walthamstow and East Ham were about average, Leyton Council tried to rid themselves of a loss-making operation by leasing it to the LCC, the South Metropolitan Tramways were sustained by the profits of their power supply business, Croydon Corporation considered selling out to the bus companies, the London United Tramways spent several years in receivership, and Barking Council gave up tramway operation in 1929.

24. *'Feltham' prototype car no.331 was fitted with a central entrance and exit, a configuration not pursued on the production fleet. The car is posed at Fulwell early in 1930 in this official view, and is now preserved at the National Tramway Museum, Crich, Derbyshire.* MET. London Transport Museum U6893

25. *A production-series MET Feltham car at the entrance to Finchley depot. The 40 foot rigid length of the Felthams is seen clearly in this view.* GEC Traction, BTH Collection

In 1911 the London trams carried two-thirds of London's total passenger traffic. By 1921 this had fallen to one-half, and by 1927 to one-third, but these figures reflected a rapidly growing motor bus share in newly developed areas served only by buses. In actual terms the number of tramway passengers went on rising. The LCC carried 636 million in 1919, and 677 million in 1932 - 1933 (96 million of them at workmen's fares). The Metropolitan Electric carried 122 million in 1930 - 1931, about the same as in 1918 but higher than in the mid 1920s.

The capital expenditure on the LCC Tramways to 1933 was £18,866,414. By 1933 £10,891,373 of this had been repaid out of fares, and in addition £8,302,681 had been paid in interest. Repayment was a first charge on earnings, which means that the municipal tramways were subject to a stricter financial regime than the bus or railway companies. Mr C S Dunbar reckons that if they had been a joint stock company the LCC Tramway would have paid an average dividend of 5 per cent.

The main reason why the Metropolitan Electric and London United Tramways were less successful was the high road charges which they had been obliged to pay. Most of the streets traversed by the tramways had been widened or otherwise improved when the tracks were laid. The LCC charged one-tenth of street widening costs to the tramways, the total being £814,153 for 158 miles. The Middlesex County Council charged more than one-third to the Metropolitan Electric Tramways, the total being £972,457 for 53 miles, or £18,347 per mile against the LCC's £5153, or three and a half times as much. The London United had paid out quite excessive sums, which brought the total for the three companies (MET, LUT and SMET) to about £2 million.

London traffic still derives substantial benefits today from road widening carried out at the time the tramways were being laid, much of it paid for by the tramways account.

On its formation the London County Council was given £8.5 millions of London Transport stock, only £0.5 million more than the outstanding debt, and no account was taken of the depreciated but debt-free assets represented by the £10,891,373 capital that had already been repaid. This enormous write-off made it much easier for London Transport to replace the trams, indeed it could be said that the LCC trams had dug their own financial grave. Another factor was that the London Passenger Transport Act 1933 gave powers for any tramway line in London to be abandoned at one month's notice without the additional formalities normally required.

In many British cities the least financially successful tramway routes had already been replaced by municipal motor buses, but Parliament had refused to grant London municipalities the power to run buses, due to the entrenched position of the existing bus companies and particularly the London General Omnibus Company. There was no corresponding restriction on trolleybuses, and the LCC sought powers in the early 1920s for a trolleybus route from West Norwood via Crystal Palace to Catford. Croydon Corporation had considered trolleybuses for its Addiscombe route and the MET had obtained trolleybus powers for Wood Green to Walthamstow, which had lapsed [1].

In the event it was the London United Tramways who introduced trolleybuses to London, by converting their Kingston area routes in 1931. These trolleybuses were a spectacular financial success, costing 13 per cent less per mile to run and earning 26 per cent more revenue. New trolleybuses were being compared with ancient trams on worn-out track, but the financial message was too strong to ignore. If similar financial results could be achieved on other routes, they would be sufficient to write off the remaining value of the track and to pay the financial charges arising from the conversion, and still leave a profit. It was left to *Tramway and Railway World*, in its January 1932 issue, to point out that the conversion had taken place in a favourable area, where traffic flow was more evenly distributed through the working hours of the day than was generally the case on the rest of the tramway systems.

However, it was not expected that money could be found for a wholesale conversion programme, and the LPTB began to rebuild some of the South London trams in 1935. 250 cars were authorised, but only 150 were done. The rest were cancelled due to a change of policy in 1936.

This change of policy (or time-scale) foresaw the abandonment of all the London trams and their replacement by trolleybuses. It was made possible by the granting by the government of low-interest loans to relieve unemployment, and the resulting activity was known as the New Works Programme 1935 - 1940.

This provided £39 million for railway improvements and £5.2 million for trolleybuses. Further funding was made available in 1936 - 1937 and it was this that sealed the fate of the London tramways. Some of the proposed new or newly electrified railways such as Epping to Ongar, Woodford to Hainault, and the Alexandra Palace branch were rather optimistic and would probably have made more sense as tramways, but there was no precedent for this, and it was not considered.

The war brought the tramway conversion programme to a halt in 1940 and when the war ended, it was first necessary to replace London's worn-out motorbus fleet. The tramways were kept running until 1950 - 1952, which was a tribute to the robust construction of the tram fleet, but the un-modernised trams did not compare very well with the new post-war generation of buses.

In every case the arguments employed were financial. It is true that the trams were opposed by associations representing other road users, particularly private motorists, but this was **not** the main reason for their disappearance. If the trams had been substantially more profitable than buses, they might have survived and been a major stimulus to road improvements, as on the Continent.

In their last complete year (1950) the London trams took £2,360,000 in fares but cost £3,614,156 to run, leaving a deficit of £1,244,156. In 1951, with fewer trams running, the deficit was still £1,155,000. Tramway costs were rising faster than bus costs and from an actuarial standpoint the £9 million cost of the conversion programme was therefore justified. Within two years the whole London operation was in deficit, but that was the result of inflation coupled with political opposition to fare increases.

Conclusion

From the foregoing it is possible to pin-point the main reasons for the disappearance of London's tramways:

1) They were not allowed to exploit the advantages of rails properly in regard to overload capacity, automatic steering, and the operation of coupled or articulated cars. They were operated as buses on rails and not as trains in the street. Buses without rails were clearly cheaper.

2) They were saddled with an expensive and inflexible system of current collection and failed to attempt to change it until it was too late.

3) They were saddled with high financial charges for road-widening and paving which benefited their competitors. They also had to pay rates on their tracks and maintain road surfaces which were used by their competitors.

4) British tramway legislation places greater burdens on the operator than does that of most other countries.

5) The unusual division of powers in London between the regional authority and the metropolitan boroughs hindered the proper provision by the road authorities of the facilities needed by the tramways, such as reserved tracks (or tram lanes) and loading islands.

6) The Metropolitan Police based their measures of road obstruction on vehicle size and not on vehicle capacity. One tram can carry about 20 times as many people as one private car, but the police generally sided with the motorist.

7)   The government made available large amounts of cheap money for unemployment relief in the 1930s, and this was used to replace the West London and North London trams by trolleybuses in a programme which would otherwise have had to be spread over a much longer period.

8)   The legislation which brought into being the London Passenger Transport Board forced the Underground Group to sell off the North Metropolitan Electric Power Supply Co Ltd, which prior to 1930 had sustained financially the Metropolitan Electric Tramways.

It was not the tramway itself that failed in London; it was the regulations governing its use.

(1) Law Reports, Court of Appeal, 6 April, 1900
     Attorney General v. The London County Council

The London County Council have no power to carry on the business of omnibus proprietors in connexion with their tramways.

The Action was brought by the Attorney General on the relation of a large number of the omnibus proprietors of London against the LCC, seeking a declaration that it is beyond the powers of the LCC to carry on the business of omnibus proprietors in connexion with their tramways. 'Where there is an Act of Parliament creating a corporation for a particular purpose, what it does not expressly or implicitly authorise is taken to be prohibited.'

The London County Council purchased the tramways on 27 December 1898 and ran omnibuses from the south side of Blackfriars Bridge to Farringdon Street via Waterloo Bridge, Strand and Whitehall to Westminster Bridge, at a half-penny fare. The former Company only ran buses across the three bridges and back.

'I make this declaration in the terms of the claim.'

References to Chapter 3

Dunbar, C S. 'Idealism and Competition'. In *Modern Tramway,* May and June 1967

Dunbar, C S. *London's Tramway Subway.* Light Railway Transport League. Various editions

Gibbon, Sir Gwilym and R W Bell. *History of the London County Council, 1889-1939.* London, Macmillan, 1939

Murdoch, A D. *Tramway and Bus Developments in Great Britain.* Report to the Melbourne and Metropolitan Tramways Board, produced 1934 for private circulation. Includes interviews with LCC Tramways management, June 1933 (reproduced as Paper IV in this volume).

Smeeton, C S. *The Metropolitan Electric Tramways.* Light Rail Transit Association. Vol 1 1984, Vol 2 1986

Willsher, M J D. *The LCC Trailers.* Light Rail Transit Association, 1982

Tramway & Railway World, June 1932. Report of the Conference of the Tramways & Light Railways Association

Further Reading

Baddeley, G E and Oakley, E R. *Current Collection for Tramway and Trolleybus Systems.* Dartford, Nemo Productions, 1975

Barker, T C and Robbins, Michael. *A History of London Transport.* London, George Allen and Unwin. *Volume II, The Twentieth Century to 1970,* 1974

Cooper, T. *The Wheels Used to Talk to Us.* Sheffield, Tallis Publishing, 1977

Day, John R. *London's Trams and Trolleybuses.* London Transport, 1977

Graves, Charles. *London Transport Carried On.* LPTB, 1947

Green, Oliver and Reed, John. *The London Transport Golden Jubilee Book.* Daily Telegraph, 1983

Guilmartin, G Harry. *Bare Empty Sheds.* Tramway and Light Railway Society, 1986

'Kennington'. *London County Council Tramways Handbook.* Tramway and Light Railway Society, 3rd ed, 1977

Summerfield, Vernon. *London Transport.* LPTB, 1935

Tramway and Railway World, 9 March 1933. Description of 74-seat centre-entrance trolleybus for London United Tramways, the first to equal the capacity of a `tramcar.

Willoughby, D W and Oakley, E R. *London Transport Tramways Handbook.* Dartford, authors, 1972

Wilson, B G. *London United Tramways.* George Allen and Unwin, 1971

4 LONDON COUNTY COUNCIL TRAMWAYS: Melbourne Tramway Manager's Visit, 1933

A D Murdoch

I interviewed Mr Thomas, General Manager of the London County Council Tramways, now taken over by the London Transport Board. He was in the throes of transfer and reorganisation.

He is of the opinion that there is still room for up-to-date tram services where the traffic warrants the cost. For heavy traffic and close headways, trams are still superior. He considers that some of the smaller tramways, especially those with single line and loops should never have been built. Economically they were unsound, and with the narrow streets and the limited area served, they could never hope to pay.

With respect to the larger tramways, he thought that many had permitted routes to drift into a hopeless position by allowing their equipment, tracks, etc, to get into an acute state of disrepair, making a comparison with buses odious, and giving the buses a superior claim not justified by their merits. It was unreasonable to compare buses a few months old with trams over 30 years of age, with tracks to match. For mass transportation, however, they had proved that there was no superior instrument to the tramway, and with further cross-town connections, their status was capable of being improved.

The London City Council Tramways are handicapped by one route only through to the City, the Kingsway Shallow Subway. This connects the North London tramway services with the south via the Thames Embankment. The subway was enlarged to make it available for double-deck cars. It was closed during the progress of the work, and buses were substituted for trams to maintain the services. The passenger movement decreased, however, and the service had to be reduced until the completion of the work. The interesting fact is that, when the subway was completed and the larger cars routed through, not only did the traffic return, but with the greater capacity of the double decker, there was an increase of 3d per mile in the revenue, thoroughly justifying the expenditure of £300,000.

Mr Thomas said that a connecting route over Blackfriar's Bridge would be just as successful as the Kingsway Route. Possibly, with the new Transport Board, this desirable connection may be brought about, although the City authorities are against it.

It is not, however, easy to draw definite conclusions from this experience. Passengers by bus had to change from one vehicle to another, and the journey was subject to street traffic conditions compared with through-running trams, larger and more comfortable vehicles and no traffic interference whilst running through the Shallow Subway.

The London County Council have been one of the most progressive tramway concerns in England, and they have kept their track, rolling stock and equipment in a state of efficiency. They have suffered a great deal from duplication of services, especially competition with the buses run by the London General Omnibus Company (now of the same Board). In many cases, these services were justified by their promoters on the basis of feeding areas and settlements beyond the terminal points of the tramways and then paralleling the tramway routes in the densely populated sections already adequately provided for.

Competition has forced the LCC to improve their rolling stock and speed up their service, bus and coach developments setting the pace. Mr Thomas tells his engineering section they should discontinue their 25 to 30 years' practice and build trams for a life of not more than 12 years, as obsolescence is a more important factor than depreciation. His instructions to the PW Department are that they must set about making their tracks suitable for the general increase in speeds necessary to meet the demands for service and competition.

The LCC have increased their average speed including stops and standing time, from 8.4 miles to 10.14 miles per hour. He instanced the effect of improved speed on traffic on the Croydon section. This line was previously run by a Company, and average speed was 7.5 miles per hour. Through-running arrangements were made, and the average speed was increased to 10.5 miles per hour, and the traffic at once improved.

Conduit

London has, undoubtedly, been handicapped by the conduit system, there being not only the heavy initial expenditure, but the higher maintenance charges too. They have about 120 route miles of conduit tramways, and Mr Thomas informed me that their operating expenses were approximately £140,000 per annum more for the conduit than for the corresponding length of the overhead trolley system - that is over £1,000 per mile per annum in maintenance charges, apart from the higher capital costs. They would be glad to get rid of this incubus, and, when the day for renewals arrives, it is possible that, under the new authority, there will be some effort to do so. Their experience endorses the action of the Board in deciding to eliminate the conduit system from consideration when dealing with the conversion of the cable lines.

Revenue and Fares

Sunday and holiday traffic has decreased. As an instance of this, he stated that on August Bank Holiday, the maximum revenue in the old days was in the order of £19,000 for the day. This has fallen to about £13,000 for the day.

Several fare schemes have been tried out with the object of improving the revenue. They have tried a 2d all-the-way ticket on Sundays. Subsequently this was increased to 3d with 5d return. Now the experiment is 1/- all day and 6d after 6 pm. In his opinion, none of these schemes has increased the revenue.

Employment and Training of Men

I inspected the Depots, etc, with Mr Geary, the Traffic Superintendent of the LCC Tramways.

Their employment and training methods are closely allied with ours. A great deal of care is exercised in choosing the right type of man for the job to make quite sure he is temperamentally suited for transport work. No person is selected for a driver's position unless he has had previous experience as a driver of a horse or motor vehicle.

With respect to conductors: it is not customary to promote them to drivers' positions. The lighter man is selected for the work. The two classes are kept separate. Their view is that the qualities required for driving and conducting work are not identical. A good conductor may not necessarily make a good driver.

With the improved air brakes now being used, a lighter man can do driving work than was previously the case when hand brakes, except on emergency occasions, were solely used for braking purposes. The promotion, therefore, from the position of conductor to driver is, in our case, quite justified, provided the man is temperamentally suitable for the job. Precautions are necessary before making the transfer.

The LCC men are required to pass a medical inspection, and if applicants are considered satisfactory, they are put into a training school and are passed into the service. There is no resident Medical Officer, and there is no system of periodical examination, but Mr Geary thought it would be an advantage to have one.

In our training, we have a follow-up system after the man has passed through the school. Whilst we do not expect men taking up duties as a driver to have had previous driving experience, our preliminary enquiries and studies help us to eliminate the temperamentally unsuitable.

I discussed with Mr Geary tests which were being applied in Paris and Berlin to ensure the elimination of temperamentally unsuitable men for traffic work. He informed me that they had closely studied these methods, but were satisfied that they were by no means perfect, and their investigations had shown that the Paris and Berlin men selected by these methods were just as accident-prone as their own men, and no better results were achieved.

Working Rosters

In working the rosters, the motormen and conductors are paired, and they work continuously together until the new roster is posted. Our practice is contrary to this. The motormen and conductors work round the roster in opposite directions, thus at each weekly change, the same two men are not in charge of the car, and this practice is found to have worked satisfactorily.

Conductors' Change

Conductors are provided with 3/6d change money which must be turned in and checked each night and morning.

Assistant Conductors

Mr Geary said that they had many investigations into the subject of missed fares, arising out of complaints from Councillors, and assistant conductors had been used at peak periods. Their present practice, however, was to eliminate as far as possible, all assistants, and a few only were used on the Thames Embankment. They found a single conductor could work a double-deck car as effectively as with an assistant. Gossiping was less, and, if odd fares were missed, it was less expensive than the extra men.

Dismissals and Punishments

The District Superintendents have right of discharge up to motormen with not more than 17 years' service. There is, however, no Appeal Board such as we have in Australia. Those dissatisfied with the decision of the District Superintendent may appeal to the Traffic Superintendent, and from him to the General Manager. They seem to work in harmony with the men's union. Union officers do not spend as much of their time in the works and departments as they do here.

Ticket Printing

The London County Council is one of the few authorities that does its own ticket printing. They have a factory equipped for the purpose. Roll paper is used, and two rotary machines do the work.

The rolls are first cut into widths equal to four tickets. The second process is that of colouring them. Aniline dyes are used, and a rotary press of their own design does the colouring work. It is quite simple. Metal rollers dip into a trough containing the dye and the paper is pressed between these and other rollers in such a manner as to leave two coloured bands on each side of the ticket, with a clear space between them. Various denominations of tickets are indicated by this system of colouring.

The tickets are printed four at a time, and checking is done every 50 sheets, but notwithstanding this, errors do occur. The records are so kept that, in case of need, they can trace the person responsible.

Including the overhead charges which, they say, are fairly heavy, the tickets average 6d per 1000. As many of these are longer than ours and the paper is 0.013 of an inch in thickness, this cost appears to be reasonable. Outside tramways are paying up to 8d per 1000. Our costs in Melbourne are 5^{11}_{16}d per 1000, with advertisements, and 5^{7}_{16}d without, but our tickets are 2.5" x 1.5" compared with 4.5" long for some of the London tickets, and the thickness of our tickets is 0.0025 inches. We make them up in lots of 200, whereas they make them up in bundles of 50. Our tickets are not suitable for the bell punch.

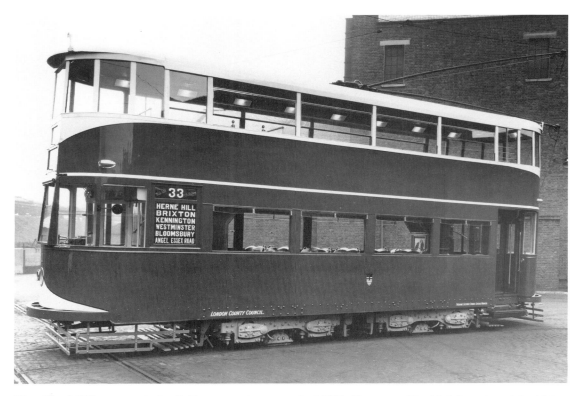

26.   *The LCC's answer to the Felthams was its car no.1 of 1932. Known as* Bluebird *from its original blue and cream livery, no.1 was 36 feet long, some four feet shorter than its MET/LUT contemporaries, but seated 66 to the Feltham's 64 passengers. No further examples were built, but* Bluebird *herself has survived to join the collection of the National Tramway Museum at Crich.*   LCC

27.   *Top deck interior of LCC no.1, showing the upholstered bi-directional seats.*

LCC. London Transport Museum 25133

Conductors' Ticket Boxes

Tickets are made up at a central office and distributed to the Depots for use. Cardboard trays with the returned stocks of tickets etc, are placed on a continuous belt as it moves along the ticket room. Girls are stationed at intervals, and as the trays pass, they add stock for the following day's work, and enter it on the journal. One girl adds 1d tickets, another 2d tickets and third 3d tickets, and so on, each doing her share of the work as the belt moves. By the time a tray has reached the end of the room, the work is complete, and the tickets put into the box ready for delivery to the Depot. A great deal of ingenuity has been displayed in developing this system. It runs smoothly and well, and they are proud of the achievement, but I could not help thinking that much of the work might have been done at the Depots at less cost.

The bigger tramways such as Glasgow, Manchester and the London United and the London General Omnibus Company decentralise their ticket work as we do, and I should say to the advantage of the system as a whole. However, no costs were available for direct comparison.

Holloway Depot

With Mr Geary, inspected the Holloway Depot, which houses about 300 cars. A transfer table is used for stalling them. The man in charge of the transfer table acts as despatcher, and controls both cars running into and out of service.

Car Washing

They have abandoned the practice of washing cars by running them through a water screen. They use special nozzle sprays with water at 250-300 lbs pressure. In connection therewith, the men use brushes and these, they say, have improved the quality of the work.

Tools etc On Car

Each car carries a 5-ton jack and tool box with hammer, tools, etc. This box is sealed, and, in case of emergency, the seals are broken, but the men in charge must report the case.

New Car

The new car is run from this Depot. It represents their answer to bus competition and the demand for luxury. The colour scheme is blue and white, inside and out. Reversible cushion and spring seats on both upper and lower decks, with observation windows which can be raised and lowered by pressure applied to a pad in the centre of the frame. The windows are balanced and move easily. The motorman is housed in a special cabin to which the public has not access. In this cabin, there are the usual gadgets, controllers, car brakes interlocked with track magnet shoes, etc.

Hackney Depot, Telephone Traffic Control

Inspected the telephone control room for the northern section. Some years ago, they installed at this Depot a Western Electric system of telephone control. This is connected to the street boxes which can be used by the traffic staff, including inspectors, motormen and conductors. Any one of the telephone boxes can ring the central control, and the operator in charge can connect any box with any other on the system. Up to seventeen telephone stations can be connected with one line.

They have found the system of control of great advantage to them in their work of maintaining headways. In the case of trouble, the control is informed, and, from this point every part of the system can be communicated with. Mr Geary said that, if they were installing the system again, there would be fewer stations per mile, as in case of serious disorganisation, they experienced congestion.

Cars

Mr Sinclair is the Rolling Stock Superintendent. The shops are used for repairs to the whole of their rolling stock, numbering 1,712.

A small number of trams only is provided with motormen's shields. The Police Department objected that drivers could not control their cars so effectively with glass shields as without them. This embargo has now been removed.

The maximum traction truck is largely used, although they now definitely favour equal wheel bogie equipment as being more suitable for heavy work.

Their latest cars have 26.5" wheels, and these wheels will be standard on all equipment. They favour the smaller diameter wheel as it permits of improved car construction, and is advantageous for high speed, lightweight motors. It is not, however, proposed to scrap any of the existing types. They cannot afford to do this.

Wheels are ground, the treads are finished to a taper of 1 in 10, contemplate going to 1 in 15, although the average angle of worn treads is in the order of 1 in 7. They appear to give more attention to the condition of the flanges than the treads. So long as a wheel has sound flanges, the treads may take care of themselves. To prevent loose tyres slipping off, they turn a slight groove on the opposite side to lip, and, after shrinking on the tyre, burr over with a pneumatic riveting tool.

Springs

They are using leaf springs on their truck mountings as they give smoother riding qualities. This is the experience in Melbourne.

Motors etc

All new motor equipments are provided with roller bearings. Although they have many advantages, these are not so apparent when mixed with other equipment at a Depot. They have ceased to use split gear wheels and solid helical gears are now in use. Many experiments have been made with motor mountings to get as much weight spring borne as possible.

Trucks etc

About 60 cars were provided with a radial slot and block for the axle, but these did not give the satisfactory results predicted for them. They had to correct the design. Roller bearing trucks are also being used, and, to eliminate horn blocks, and lessen noise, the axle boxes are connected with the trucks by a radial arm, and a wearing plate takes the side thrust. This is the EMB type made by the Electro-Mechanical Brake Co, West Bromwich.

Brakes

They are testing out combined air and electric track brakes on their newest cars, the results so far being satisfactory.

Seats

All cars are now fitted with cushion seats. Mr Sinclair said that competition had forced them to pay more attention to comfort. Motor buses were doing so, and people looked for it. Spring seats are used, and moquette is favoured, although not so hygienic as leather. Rubber is being tried out, but there is not sufficient experience to say definitely what the results are likely to be. The traffic does not look with a kindly eye on them.

Mr Geary does not share the opinion with a number of other transport authorities that rubber seats are the best. He favours springs, being more resilient and giving greater comfort to passengers. Tramways have been forced into improving their seats by motor coach and motor car users. Wooden or slat seats are a thing of the past.

In their effort to improve the seating accommodation of the cars, old seats are being suitably covered with cushions and upholstered to match the interiors of the cars. They are not scrapping the material of their old seats. Everything that can be conveniently used in the converted seat is pressed in service.

A car has been equipped on the lower deck with the Peter's reversible seats. These are a luxury pattern, the seats being mounted on a centre pin. They are reversed by pressing a foot lever, and turning them round. The operation is simple, and there appears to be little to get out of order. Experience however, will show up the weak spots.

Destination Signs and Car Notices

Route and destination signs are stencilled by the silk screen process, and the same is used for painting side destination bars, as in our own shops.

Car notices are printed in red and black on white paper. These are fixed in suitable positions and varnished over. They make a particularly neat finish, cheaper than the metal signs, and easily replaced in case of damage, and, as the cars are brought in once every twelve months for painting, the notices are replaced.

Painting

The standard colour for the LCC cars on the outside is vermilion. This does not, however, apply to the interiors. They have no fixed colour scheme. The practice is to paint 150 cars or so of a colour, and give the passenger the idea of change in tramway practice.

The painting costs about £16 per car, 80 man hours for the inside and 75 for the outside. The job is done in 155 working hours or thereabouts, and ten men are used on the job, which includes cleaning and washing down, one coat of vermilion and varnish painting inside, with white enamel on the ceiling.

Cars to be painted are routed through the shops on a forward movement plan. For this purpose, a steel rope haulage system is used. The trams are connected to this, and progress forward at the rate of three inches per minute. As a tram goes forward, the various classes of work are attended to by men stationed at intervals along the route. As the tram goes into the drying room at the far end, the last touch of varnish is given to it. It is left in the drying room overnight, the temperature being over 70 degrees, with hot air delivered in ducts below the roof.

Trams are painted every year, and overhauled every two years, irrespective of mileage. At the overhaul period, cars are washed as they enter the works. They are then run under an electric crane. The old trucks are removed, and the body goes to the paint shop. The body repairs, unless extensive, are also done on the continuous movement plan.

Foundry Work

The LCC does quite a lot of foundry work. Motor gear cases are cased in aluminium alloy. Motor bearings are brass castings, mostly done in their own shops. CI journal boxes are also cast in their own foundry. Machine moulding is used and they have an up-to-date drying oven.

The armature shop is particularly busy, old equipment providing plenty of work. They have increased the capacity of some armatures by rewinding with rectangular wire coils, asbestos insulated.

28. *Tube/tram co-ordination and competition. MET class C1 car no.196 amid construction work at Turnpike Lane Station, early in 1932, showing the tram loading islands with direct stairways to the station. Turnpike Lane Station opened as part of the Piccadilly underground railway extension from Finsbury Park to Arnos Grove on 19 September 1932, providing competition (officially 'relief') to the trams between Kings Cross, Finsbury Park and Wood Green. The car is on route 34, Alexandra Palace/Muswell Hill–Bruce Grove. Trams ran along Priory Road and into Alexandra Park, but did not climb the steep Muswell Hill itself.* Fox Photos. London Transport Museum 25125

29. *The beginning of the end for London's trams. London Transport class T car no.2320, built for London United Tramways in 1906, at Hammersmith on route 89 (Acton–Hammersmith), during the erection of overhead wiring for trolleybuses, which replaced the trams in 1936.* LPTB. London Transport Museum 25124

A number of vacuum drying and impregnating machines were being used. Mr Sinclair was at one time the engineer of the English Electric Company's factory, and is an expert on traction motors. He was enthusiastic on the subject of the application of asbestos to armature and field coil conductors. In place of cotton covered wire what may be described as a fire-proof material, asbestos, is now being used. It permits of higher temperatures and higher rating of machines, and has proved of great assistance in adding to the capacity of old equipment.

Breakdowns

One of the best breakdown trucks I have seen was that recently designed by the LCC. It is a heavy petrol vehicle and is provided with buffers for pushing and a chain for towing disabled trams. It has a five-ton crane, hydraulic jacks and gadgets for dealing with trucks with broken axles, raising heavy vehicles, and, if necessary, for clearing a breakdown from the road, whether occasioned by the Council's own equipment or vehicles belonging to other people. Traffic men are in charge of this car, though they were given training in the workshops. It is considered that, with their knowledge of the road and service conditions, they are better suited to the work than others. Mr Geary kindly supplied me with a blue print of this and photographs.

In connection with delays, periodical conferences between the Officers of the traffic and the rolling stock branch are held. All traffic delays are discussed, and an effort made to find a cause and to prevent a recurrence.

Advertising

The London County Council Tramway Department is one of the most active advertisers. They use the poster, guide book and car notice for this purpose. London is in a specially advantageous position for publicity work. There is a large floating population and so many attractions, historical places and buildings suitable for poster treatment. The Tramways have their own printing department. In this section, certain classes of poster work as well as the smaller notices, are produced.

London County Council have a tramway map and timetable, a folder similar to that which we issued a few years ago. On one side, there is a map of the tramway system with route numbers to assist passenger in selecting their cars, and, on the reverse, timetables of first and last cars.

The map and timetable is distributed at the offices or by inspectors or regulators free of charge. Conductors do not carry them.

As things might have been. London's only fully reserved track tramway was the roadside reservation beside Whipps Cross Road, from Whipps Cross to Leytonstone. Running along the edge of Epping Forest, much of the reservation is still discernable. Track was still visible in places at least up to the 1960s. Subsequently, part of the route has been gravelled or turned into car parking areas.

30. An ex Walthamstow car heads westbound on route 61, en route for Leyton, Baker's Arms, in 1939.

D A Thompson

31. East and westbound cars passing. Note the single combined overhead supports and lamp post.

Photographer unknown

TRAMWAY ROUTES MAP AND GUIDE

TRAMWAYS

METROPOLITAN ELECTRIC LONDON UNITED SOUTH METROPOLITAN ELECTRIC

ISSUED FREE.

LONDON'S UNDERGROUND

THE METROPOLITAN ELECTRIC TRAMWAYS. LTD.—continued.

PLACES OF INTEREST ON THE SYSTEM.

	Route No.
GOLF COURSES:	
Bush Hill Park (Enfield)	26, 29
Edgware (Canons Park)	66
Enfield	26, 29
Hampstead (Hampstead Heath)	40, 60
Hendon	54, 66
Highgate..	9, 19, 69
Horsendon Hill (Sudbury)	62
Muswell Hill	32, 34, 51
Neasden	54, 66
North Middlesex (Totteridge).. ..	19
South Herts. (Totteridge)	19
HISTORIC BUILDINGS:	
Edmonton Old Church and Lamb's Cottage	27, 49, 59, 79
Enfield Church and Remains of Royal Palace	26, 29
Theobald's and Old Temple Bar	79
Waltham Abbey and Cross	79
Whitchurch (Church of Handel, and Wm. Powell, the Harmonious Blacksmith) ..	66
RAILWAY TERMINI:	
Euston (L.M.S.R.)	19, 27, 29, 53, 69
Fenchurch Street (L.M.S.R.)	53, 71
Holborn Viaduct (Southern R.)	21, 59, 79
King's Cross (L.N.E.R.)	21, 59
Liverpool Street (L.N.E.R.)	49
Marylebone (L.N.E.R.)	60, 62
Paddington (G.W.R.)	60, 62
St. Pancras (L.M.S.R.)	21, 59
THEATRES & MUSIC HALLS:	
Alexandra, Stoke Newington	49
Collins', Islington	9, 51, 39, 79
Finsbury Park Empire	21, 27, 29, 53, 39, 59, 79
Golders Green Hippodrome	40, 60
Holborn Empire (2 mins. from Bloomsbury)	21, 51, 59
Islington Empire	9, 51, 39, 79
Metropolitan	60, 62
New Hippodrome, Harlesden.. ..	60, 62
The Bedford	19, 27, 29, 53, 69
The Regent (" Euston "), King's Cross ..	21, 59
Shoreditch Empire	49
West End Theatres (near Bloomsbury) ..	51
Wood Green Empire	21, 29, 39, 34
VARIOUS:	
Alexandra Park, Palace and Racecourse ..	32, 34, 51
Caledonian Market	21, 27, 29, 53, 59
Hampstead Garden City	40, 60
Ladbroke Hall	60, 62
Royal Agricultural Hall	9, 51, 39, 79
Zoological Gardens	19, 27, 29, 53, 69

THE LONDON UNITED TRAMWAYS, LIMITED—continued.

Route No.	Route.	Journey Times, Intervals, Fares.
71	**Hampton Court & Wimbledon** Via Hampton Court Road, Kingston Bridge, Clarence Street, Cambridge Road, Kingston Road, New Malden, West Barnes Lane, Raynes Park, Worple Road.	Time 44 mins. Interval : Wkdays 6 mins. Sundays 8 mins. Fare 6d.
73	**Kingston Hill & The Dittons** Via London Road, Eden Street Kingston, Penrhyn Road, Claremont Road, Victoria Road, Brighton Road, Portsmouth Road.	Time 27 mins. Interval : Wkdays 10 mins. Sundays 10 mins. Fare 3d.
77	**Tolworth & Richmond Park Gates** Via Ewell Road, Victoria Road, Claremont Road, Penrhyn Road, Eden Street Kingston, Richmond Rd., King's Road.	Time 27 mins. Interval : Wkdays 10 mins. Sundays 10 mins. Fare 3d.
	(Additional Cars work between Kingston (Eden Street) and Tolworth during week-day evening rush hours.)	Time 22 mins. Interval : Wkdays 10 mins. Fare 2d.
	(Additional Cars work between Surbiton Station and Kingston Eden Street on Saturday afternoon and evening only.)	Time 10 mins. Interval : Sat. afternoons & evenings 12 mins. Fare 1d.
81	**Summerstown & Haydons Rd. Junct.** Via Plough Lane, Haydons Road.	Time 8 mins. Interval : Wkdays 20 mins. Sundays 20 mins. Fare 1½d.
89	**Acton & Hammersmith** Via Acton Vale, Askew Road, Paddenswick Road, King Street Hammersmith.	Time 19 mins. Interval : Wkdays 4 mins. Sundays 5 mins. Fare 3d.
	Part Service extended to Southall on Saturday afternoons and evenings	Time 48 mins. Interval 8 mins. Fare 7d.
	Acton & Putney Extension of above route on week-days via Fulham Palace Road.	Time 34 mins. Interval : Wkdays 8 mins. Fare 5d.
2 4	**Wimbledon Hill & Victoria Embankment** Via Merton Road, Tooting Broadway, Balham High Road, Clapham Road, Kennington Gate, Westminster Bridge. **Hampton Court & Victoria Embankment** Extension of the above routes via same roads as Route 71 on Saturday afternoons and on Sundays from May to mid-October only.	Time 58 mins. Interval : Wkdays 3 mins. Fare 5d. Time 99 mins. Interval : Sat. aft. 12 mins. Sundays 8 mins. Fare 11d.

Extracts from contemporary publicity.

The London bus map has a long pedigree, the format of these prewar examples (reduced for reproduction) being immediately recognisable.

Above: Underground group company tramways, 1.1.1929, with extracts for LUT routes and places of interest served by MET.

Below: London Transport, issue no.1, 1940, of what has now become a combined trolleybus and tram map. 58 trolleybus and 41 tram routes were listed, together with 4 all-night trolleybus services and 6 night tram routes. The night services were aimed at workers, and did not operate on Saturday nights. Prices are now excluded from the summary information for each route. Details for routes 31.33.34 and 35 are reproduced here.

TROLLEYBUS & TRAM MAP

---

31 BATTERSEA Princes Head - ISLINGTON GREEN
Via Vauxhall, Albert Embankment, Westminster Bridge, KINGSWAY SUBWAY, Bloomsbury, Rosebery Avenue

	WEEKDAYS				SUNDAY	
	First	Last	Sat.		First	Last
Time 42 mins.	6 0	11 0	11 22	Battersea, Princes Head, to Islington Green	×21	11 49
	6 0	12 10	12 30	Battersea, Princes Head, to Bloomsbury	×21	11 49
Service 5–10 mins.	6 44	11 23	11 44	Islington Green to Battersea, Princes Head	9 4	11 4
	5 22	11 34	11 55	Bloomsbury to Battersea, Princes Head	7 46	11 14
	6 44	11 52	12 19	Islington Green to Westminster	9 4	12 34

33 WEST NORWOOD MANOR HOUSE STATION
Via Herne Hill, Brixton, Kennington, Westminster Bridge, KINGSWAY SUBWAY, Bloomsbury, Angel, Essex Road, Green Lanes

	WEEKDAYS				SUNDAY	
	First	Last	Sat.		First	Last
Time 68 mins.	4 51	12 7	12 3	West Norwood to Bloomsbury	8 26	11 26
	4 51	11 15	11 20	West Norwood to Manor House	8 26	11 2
Service 5–10 mins.	5 22	12 7	12 7	Westminster to Manor House	8 55	11 33
	5 12	11 48	11 16	Manor House to West Norwood	8 23	11 16
	5 12	11 48	11 44	Manor House to Westminster	8 23	11 16

34 CHELSEA Kings Road BLACKFRIARS*
Via Battersea Bridge, Falcon Road, Clapham Junction, Lavender Hill, Clapham Common, Stockwell Road, Brixton, Coldharbour Lane, Camberwell, Elephant, Blackfriars Bridge

* Alternate Cars operate to Camberwell Green only during certain hours

	WEEKDAYS				SUNDAY	
	First	Last	Sat.		First	Last
Time 58 mins.	5 8	11 13	11 10	Chelsea to Embankment	8 47	10 55
	5 8	12 38	12 34	Chelsea to Camberwell Green	8 47	12 1
Service 5–8 mins.	5 41	11 30	11 35	Embankment to Chelsea	8 45	11 30
	4 28	12 34	12 30	Camberwell Grn. to Clapham Junc.	7 24	12 23
	5 8	12 49	12 44	Clapham Junc. to Camberwell Grn.	8 16	12 58

35 FOREST HILL - HIGHGATE STATION (Und.)
Via Brockley Rise, Crofton Park, Brockley Stn., New Cross, Peckham, Camberwell Green, Elephant, Westminster Bridge, Victoria Embankment, KINGSWAY SUBWAY, Bloomsbury, Angel, Upper Street, Highbury, Holloway

	WEEKDAYS				SUNDAY	
	First	Last	Sat.		First	Last
Time 85 mins.	6 32	12 15	11 54	Forest H. Stn. to H'gate (Archway T.)	6 25	12 0
	6 32	1 3	12 57	Forest Hill Stn. to Camberwell Grn.	6 25	12 36
Service 6–10 mins.	5 48	11 36	11 29	H'gate (Archway T.) to Forest H. Stn.	5 34	10 35
	5 48	12 22	12 33	Highgate (Archway T.) to Camb. Grn.	5 34	12 12

ALL-NIGHT TRAMS
(Saturday Nights excepted)

POPLAR Blackwall Tunnel BLOOMSBURY
Via East India Dock Road, Commercial Road, Shoreditch, Great Eastern Street, Old Street, Clerkenwell Road.

Blackwall Tunnel ..	11 46	12 10	1 10	1 40	2 40	3 5	4 17	4 44	..	..	..	..
Gardiners Corner ..	12	1 29	1 59	2 59	3 23	4 36	5 2	..	..	..	..
Shoreditch	12 7	12 34	1 34	2 4	4 3	4 28	4 40	5 6	..	..	..
Bloomsbury {Arr.	12 21	12 51	1 51	2 21	3 21	3 45	4 54	5 21	..	..	..
{Dep.	12 24	12 54	1 54	2 24	3 24	3 42	4 12	5 12	5 42	..	..
Shoreditch	12 41	1 12	2 11	2 42	3 42	4 12	4 30	5 0	5 59	..	..
Gardiners Corner ..	12 46	1 17	2 16	2 47	3 47	4 17	5 17	5 47	..	..	..
Blackwall Tunnel ..	1 6	1 36	2 36	3 5	4 7	4 36	5 35	6 5	..	..	..

BATTERSEA Princes Head BLACKFRIARS
Via Vauxhall, Westminster Bridge

Battersea (Princes Head) ..	1	1	2	3	3 4	4 3	..	..	..	..	..
Vauxhall ..	1 16	2 18	3 18	4 18	..	..	..	..	..	..
Blackfriars {Arr.	1 31	2 32	3 32	4 32	..	..	..	..	..	..
{Dep.	1 32	2 33	3 33	4 33	..	..	..	..	..	..
Vauxhall ..	1 47	2 47	3 47	4 47	..	..	..	..	..	..
Battersea (Princes Head) ..	2 2	3 2	4 2	5 2	..	..	..	..	..	..
Wandsworth High St. ..				5 10	..	..	..	..	..	..

CLAPHAM JUNCTION WESTMINSTER STATION
Via Vauxhall, Lambeth Palace Road

Clapham Junction ..	1 59	2 50	3 45	4 39	..	..	..	..	..	..
Queens Road ..	2 4	2 55	3 50	4 44	..	..	..	..	..	..
Vauxhall ..	2 18	3 9	..	..	..	..	..	..	..	..
Westminster {Arr.	2 23	3 14	4 9	..	..	..	..	..	..	..
{Dep.	2 24	3 17	4 12	..	..	..	..	..	..	..
Vauxhall ..	2 33	3 26	4 21	..	..	..	..	..	..	..
Queens Road ..	2 43	3 36	4 31	4 45	..	..	..	..	..	..
Clapham Junction ..	2 48	3 41	4 36	4 50	..	..	..	..	..	..

TOOTING BROADWAY VICTORIA EMBANKMENT Circle
Via Streatham, Brixton, Kennington, Westminster, Blackfriars, Elephant & Castle

Tooting Broadway ..			1 13	1 43	2 13	2 43	3 13	3 43	4 13	4 43	..	..
Streatham Library ..			1 26	1 56	2 26	2 56	3 26	3 56	4 26	4 56	..	..
Kennington	12*16	12*46	1*16	1 46	2 16	2 47	3 0	3 17	4 17	4 30	5 0	5 16
Victoria Embankment	12 30	1 0	1 30	2 0	2 35	3 0	3 35	4 5	4 35	5 5	5 35
Elephant & Castle	12 35	1 5	1 35	2 5	2 35	3 5	3 35	4 5	4 35	5 5	5 35
Elephant & Castle	12 43	1 13	1 43	2 13	2 43	3 13	3 43	4 13	4 43	5 13	5 43
Kennington	12 50	1 20	1 50	2 20	2 50	3 20	3 50	4 20	4 50	5 20	5 50
Streatham Library ..	1 9	1 39	2 9	2 39	3 9	3 39	4 9	4 39	5 9	5 39	6 9
Tooting Broadway ..	1 23	1 53	2 23	2 53	3 23	3 53	4 23	4 53	5 23	5 53	6 23

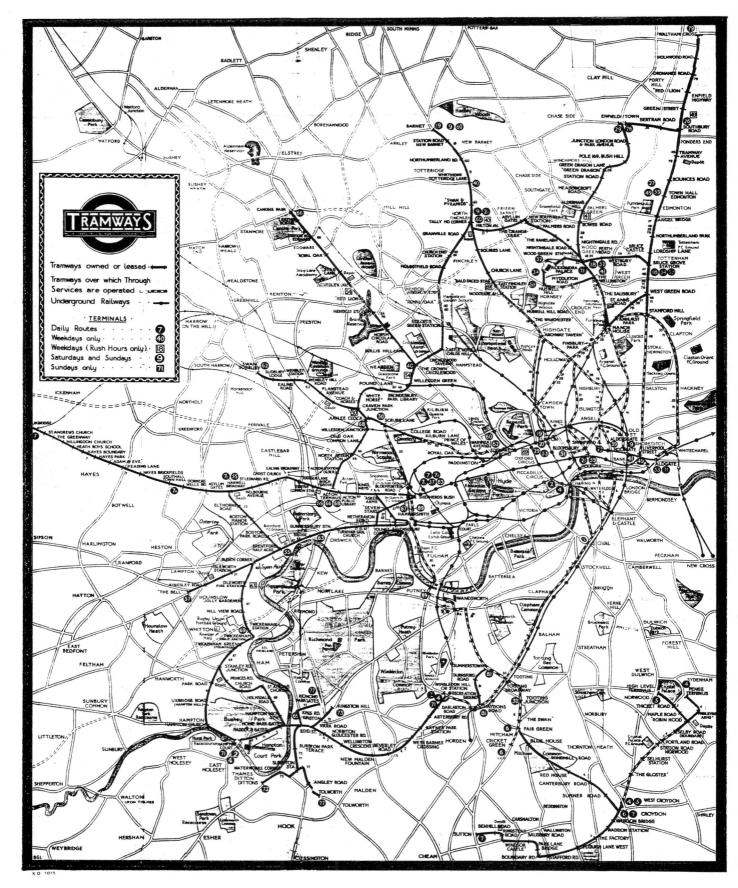

Underground Group Tramways map, 1929. Original 18″ x 15″, printed in four colours. Only group tram routes are shown, together with operations over LCC and councils' tracks. LCC route 6, Mitcham-Embankment, is however shown.